FAITH ADIELE, KELLI RUSSELL AGODON, KWAME ALEXANDER, ALISTAIR BANE, MISHA BERSON, ROBIN BLACK, RICHARD BLANCO, LOGAN BLANTON, JENNA BLUM, GAYLE BRANDEIS, SOMMER BROWNING, CASTRO LUNA, EWA CHRUSCIEL, MEG WAITE C SERENA CHOPRA, ANDREA COLLIER, GREG COLU SARAH DOMET, ANDRE DUBUS III, TERI ELAM, W. FLAME, ANA HEBRA FLASTER, JAMIE FORD, GINA FRANGELLO, JULIE GARDNER, NIKKI GIOVANNI, MICHELLE GOODMAN, DEBORAH GREEN, LISE HAINES, SADIA HASSAN, JENNIFER HAUPT, CHRISTINE HEMP, SUSAN HENDERSON, PATRICIA HENLEY, JANE HIRSHFIELD, PAM HOUSTON, MAJOR JACKSON, SCOTT JAMES, SONORA JHA, MARGOT KAHN, JESSICA KEENER, KATHLEEN KENNETH, LENA KHALAF TUFFAHA, STEPHEN P. KIERNAN, ESON KIM, SALLY KOSLOW, JEAN KWOK, DEVI S. LASKAR, ADA LIMÓN, CAROLINE LEAVITT, ROBERTO LOVATO, REBECCA MABANGLO-MAYOR, SHANA MAHAFFEY, CATHERINE MATTHEWS, DONNA MISCOLTA, DINTY W. MOORE, JANUARY GILL O'NEIL, PAULETTE PERHACH, MCKENNA PRINCING, RUBEN QUESADA, ANNA QUINN, PETER G. QUINN, DAWN RAFFEL, SUSAN RICH, MOLLY RINGLE, ELIZABETH ROSNER, JENNIFER ROSNER, KEVIN SAMPSELL, SANDRA SARR, DANI SHAPIRO, DAVID SHEFF, DAVID SHIELDS, N. L. SHOMPOLE, MICHAEL SHOU-YUNG SHUM, JENNIE SHORTRIDGE, LAURA STANFILL, DONNA BAIER STEIN, GARTH STEIN, MELISSA STUDDARD, GRACE TALUSAN, MARTHA ANNE TOLL, LUIS ALBERTO URREA, JACLYN WATTERSON, MICHELLE WILDGEN, STEVE YARBROUGH, KRISTEN MILLARES YOUNG, LIDIA YUKNAVITCH, FAITH ADIELE, KELLI RUSSELL AGODON, KWAME ALEXANDER, ALISTAIR BANE, MISHA BERSON, ROBIN BLACK, RICHARD BLANCO, LOGAN BLANTON, JENNA BLUM, GAYLE BRANDEIS, SOMMER BROWNING, ABIGAIL CARTER, CLAUDIA CASTRO LUNA, EWA CHRUSCIEL, MEG WAITE CLAYTON, CHING-IN CHEN, SERENA CHOPRA, ANDREA COLLIER, GREG COLUCCI, ELIZABETH DIMARCO, SARAH DOMET, ANDRE DUBUS III, TERI ELAM, W. RALPH EUBANKS, AMBER FLAME, ANA HEBRA FLASTER, JAMIE FORD, GINA FRANGELLO, JULIE GARDNER, NIKKI GIOVANNI, MICHELLE GOODMAN, DEBORAH GREEN, LISE HAINES, SADIA HASSAN, JENNIFER HAUPT, CHRISTINE HEMP, SUSAN HENDERSON, PATRICIA HENLEY, JANE HIRSHFIELD, PAM HOUSTON, MAJOR JACKSON, SCOTT JAMES, SONORA JHA, MARGOT KAHN, JESSICA KEENER, KATHLEEN KENNETH, LENA KHALAF TUFFAHA, STEPHEN P. KIERNAN, ESON KIM, SALLY KOSLOW, JEAN KWOK, DEVI S. LASKAR, ADA LIMÓN, CAROLINE LEAVITT, ROBERTO LOVATO, REBECCA MABANGLO-MAYOR, SHANA MAHAFFEY, CATHERINE MATTHEWS, DONNA MISCOLTA, DINTY W. MOORE, JANUARY GILL O'NEIL, PAULETTE PERHACH, MCKENNA PRINCING, RUBEN QUESADA, ANNA QUINN, PETER G. QUINN, DAWN RAFFEL, SUSAN RICH, MOLLY RINGLE, ELIZABETH ROSNER, JENNIFER ROSNER, KEVIN SAMPSELL, SANDRA SARR, DANI SHAPIRO, DAVID SHEFF, DAVID SHIELDS, N. L. SHOMPOLE, MICHAEL SHOU-YUNG SHUM, JENNIE SHORTRIDGE, LAURA STANFILL, DONNA BAIER STEIN, GARTH STEIN, MELISSA STUDDARD, GRACE TALUSAN, MARTHA ANNE TOLL, LUIS ALBERTO URREA, JACLYN WATTERSON, MICHELLE WILDGEN, STEVE YARBROUGH, KRISTEN MILLARES YOUNG, LIDIA YUKNAVITCH

D0450722

NO LONGER PROPERTY
OF ANYTHINK
RANGEVIEW LIBRARY
DISTRICT

PRAISE

"We are honored to be part of this anthology as it marks a time when this community came together in extraordinary ways."
— Pamela French, Executive Director – Book Industry Charitable Foundation

"*Alone Together* connects writers, readers, and booksellers in a wonderfully imaginative way. It's a really good book for a really good cause."
— James Patterson, Bestselling Author, and Co-Ambassador for Book Industry Charitable Foundation

"*Alone Together* showcases the human desire to grieve, explore, comfort, connect, and simply sit with the world as it weathers the pandemic ... a project that is noble in both word and deed."
— Ann Patchett, Bestselling Author, Bookseller, and Co-Ambassador for Book Industry Charitable Foundation

"These are powerful messages of unity and hope in a time of isolation and despair. *Alone Together* is a very important work that has emerged from a very dark time."
— Kevin O'Brien, *New York Times* Bestselling Author of *The Bad Sister* and *The Betrayed Wife*

"A heartening gathering of writers joining forces for community support."
— *Kirkus Reviews*

"The best kind of connection—deep, honest, steely, and humane ..."
— Gish Jen, Bestselling Author of *The Register*

A·L·O·N·E
TOGETHER

LOVE, GRIEF, AND COMFORT IN THE TIME OF COVID-19

EDITED BY JENNIFER HAUPT

central
avenue
publishing

2020

Copyright © 2020 Jennifer Haupt
Cover and internal design © 2020 Central Avenue Marketing Ltd.
Cover Design: Michelle Halket
Cover Image: Courtesy & Copyright: Creative Market
Illustrations Courtesy & Copyright: Ailsa Weisnewski

All original interviews, essays, and poetry contained herein are the property of the
original author and is printed under license to Central Avenue Marketing Ltd.

All rights reserved. No part of this book may be used or reproduced in any manner
whatsoever without written permission from the author except in the case of brief
quotations embodied in critical articles and reviews.

The views and opinions expressed herein are those of the authors and do not
necessarily reflect the viewpoints, policies, or position of Central Avenue Marketing,
its owners, business partners, or employees.

Proceeds from this book are donated to Book Industry Charitable Foundation (Binc).
All contributors and business partners are donating their time, talent, and effort.

Published by Central Avenue Publishing, an imprint of Central Avenue Marketing Ltd.
www.centralavenuepublishing.com

Published in Canada
Printed in United States of America

1. LITERARY COLLECTIONS / General   2. SELF HELP/Personal Growth

ALONE TOGETHER: Love, Grief, and Comfort in the Time of COVID-19

Trade Paperback: 978-1-77168-228-2
Epub: 978-1-77168-229-9
Mobi: 978-1-77168-230-5

1 3 5 7 9 10 8 6 4 2

CONTENTS

FOREWORD

By Garth Stein

I think a certain kind of America is doomed, though something great-
er may be coming. The novelist and only the novelist thrives on break-
down, because that's the moment when he can analyze the beauty of
the values that are falling and rising . . . One looks forward to the fall
of great civilizations because it gives us great art.

John Gardner, in an interview with Charles Johnson,

January 1973

Civilization begins with art, with the need to represent one's cul-
ture in a metaphysical way. A charcoal drawing in a cave in France,
perhaps. Music, drums, and dancing after a feast. Public discussions
and criticisms of a poem, a song, a story, a movement. A written testi-
mony of an individual's life. Because art reflects the human experience
better than any act of sustenance or preservation. An urban center is
just a crowded agora, until a can of spray paint finds itself in the hands
of a disenchanted youth . . . Then, an urban center becomes a means
of expression.

Art is the crucial element of humanity. And yet it is so easily
chucked over the side of the sinking ship when survivors are huddled
in the dark cold rain, hugging each other from fear, deciding which
of them will be eaten first, wishing they had a Hobbit along for the
journey to sing to them a song of their past . . .

The Virus moved into our world, and how did we respond? We

shut down art. Musical venues. Theatrical venues. Galleries and museums. Public open spaces, once filled with art: closed. Reading and gathering spaces, once crammed with poets: closed. Libraries and bookstores, coffee shops and bars. Even the street corners of our cities, the fanciful stages for buskers . . . closed. We threw art over the side of our sinking ship.

What an existence without art! Stranded in our homes, our mouths gagged, our hands bound, we watch our idols perform to their telephones, those hollow devices of social distance. You can see the lack of conviction in their eyes. They know best of all, though they may have forgotten in their complacency, that art is a conversation, a dialogue. Without the tangible response of a reader, a viewer, a listener, the efforts of an artist mean nothing.

They say about Seattle that there are more writers here than there are readers. I don't think this aphorism is very funny, because it would mean that we have stopped trying to understand others and are now only trying to understand ourselves. Self-reflection is good, but empathy is divine.

As a writer myself, I see the delicate nature of our literary ecosystem, and how quickly it can become imbalanced. In 2009, I cofounded Seattle7Writers, with a handful of like-minded artists who felt as I did, that we must work to support the literary ecosystem. Writers must read the work of other writers, not just their own. Writers must support the booksellers who disseminate our ideas. The librarians, the teachers, the readers. Writers must cultivate our gardens so that all can eat. Ourselves included.

I became involved with the Book Industry Charitable Foundation (Binc) two years ago because it made sense to me. Booksellers, like any of us, can fall on hard times; it is not just a moral but a fiscal imperative to ensure the well-being of a writer's main means of relevance. But it is also imperative to ensure the livelihood of our fellow citizens, those who want to engage in conversation, champions at the frontlines of our culture.

Perhaps this America is doomed. We will not know until the dust has settled. Is something greater coming, as John Gardner suggests? I don't believe that is a given, only a possibility. It is equally possible that art will remain submerged for so long, we will not be able to revive it. It is equally possible that the bottleneck of ideas will become more and more constricted until there is no more diversity, no impetus to reflect society from as many angles as possible, until we become dulled by the safety of our homes, the sway of our governments, and the colorlessness of our lives, until we don't actually care that our civilization is drawing to a close.

The writers who have contributed to this collection do care. Their ideas are flares. Their words are inspiration. They see the darkness, and they are trying to keep the flame burning. Proceeds from the sale of this volume will support Binc, and will keep booksellers selling books, will keep ideas smoldering beneath the thicket of wet leaves. One day, when the leaves have been dried by the wind that blows down from the mountain, a flame will spark to life, the leaves will burn again, and the people will have charcoal for drawing our history on the walls of our caves.

It will be a dark day, the day that art dies. Whether its death signals the beginning of the end, or the end of the beginning, or the end of the end, I do not know. But little fires are burning everywhere—including inside the pages of this book you are holding now! And so I say, do not fear the end. Pick up your pen and write. Pick up a book and read. Engage in your world; do not shrink from it. Understand that the fate of our civilization lies entirely in your hands.

GARTH STEIN is the internationally bestselling author of *The Art of Racing in the Rain*. He is the Author Leadership Circle Campaign Chair for the Book Industry Charitable Foundation.

INTRODUCTION

By Jennifer Haupt, Editor, *Alone Together*

I'm an introvert, like many writers, considering the solitude of my attic office a luxury. But I also need balance: coffee dates with friends, exchanging a smile of solidarity with the woman lifting weights next to me at the gym, and asking my local booksellers for their must-reads of the month. I depend on these daily interactions to energize me. All of these people are threads in my safety net, most without realizing it, helping to keep me buoyed above chronic, sometimes debilitating, depression. I know from experience that, too easily, staying home can turn from a luxury to a state of paralysis.

When the stay-at-home order was enacted, my connections with the outside world were frayed, as I was reduced to watching on screens as the killer virus swept through our country. Our president held press conferences declaring confidently: It will go away. I so wanted to believe him.

By the third week of quarantine, it was clear this was not going away anytime soon. Driving home this point, I received a devastating blow: the contract for my second novel was cancelled due to the plummeting economy. Of course, I wasn't the only one who lost her livelihood. Unemployment claims surpassed fifteen million and lines at understocked food banks stretched toward the horizon. Small businesses were going bankrupt by the score, forced to shut down for a few weeks, then months. No one was really sure how long it would be before they could reopen, assuming they were still solvent. This uncertainty, no end in sight, launched our entire country into a fugue-like state of shock.

Taking some kind of positive action, moving outward into the world again, became a necessity for my survival. But what could I do? I didn't have money or powerful influence, but one thing I did have was my community of writers, some of whom had launched their own fundraising and awareness campaigns against social injustice. Jessica Keener had sent me and dozens of other authors an email the past summer, asking us to donate manuscript consultation services to raise money for organizations working to stop border and detention camp abuses. The action of one person reaching out to her community, and then those people widening the circle until it included hundreds, stuck with me. (#AuthorsAgainstBorderAbuse raised $18,000 in just three months.)

The tipping point was when I saw Roxane Gay on *The Daily Show*, explaining why she tweeted an offer to give ten people $100 each, no questions asked. She said, "In a better world, the government would handle this, but we don't live in a better world."

I wanted to live in a better world.

An idea began forming, a gut feeling that energized me for the first time in weeks. Maybe I could rally authors to support the booksellers who had placed so many of our books into the hands of readers and now needed our help. Long before the pandemic hit, independent bookstores were the pillars of a worldwide literary community and the mainstays of neighborhoods across the country, providing inviting spaces to connect over ideas and coffee. My local bookstores have been a big part of my personal safety net, as well as "must visit" cultural hubs when I travel. Perhaps most important, these business owners and their employees are also pillars of a democratic society, spotlighting books you might not find elsewhere and giving marginalized people a voice through author readings and other events.

I started by putting out feelers, posting on Facebook and sending emails to authors I knew through my work as a journalist and novelist. I made a concrete, to-the-point ask: Could they contribute an essay or poem about their COVID-19 experiences to a fundraising anthology for struggling indie booksellers? Within twenty-four hours, dozens of authors were on board, and I became bolder, reaching out to a diverse range of writers I admired. During the next month, I jumped out of bed each morning, excited to see what would land in my email that day. I did not know exactly what I was creating, but every new poem and essay was a potential fragment of the soul of what I called my *Lovely Monster*.

Part of the tremendous unease during the pandemic has been recognizing that we are in the midst of transformation, with no clear sense of where it will lead and little reassuring guidance along the way. The missives arriving daily nourished me. There were stories of love triumphing over social distancing: The joy of a Zoom wedding, pandemic date night via steamy and funny texts, a mother and daughter growing closer through phone-in cooking lessons. There were also surprising, moving images of love intertwined with grief and comfort: A woman trying hard to connect with her estranged sister while social distancing, but failing. A man contemplating the comforting role of lavender in his ailing father's life, his own life, and the tumultuous history of their Latino culture. A woman professing her devotion to aloneness and realizing that her deep attractions are to nature, not humans. The poems were constructed out of possibilities: images of something new cracking open, of a glittering road, of shedding our hatred and fear like a virus.

As the pandemic stretched into May, the stories and poetry reflected the rising anxiety and anger permeating our country. One woman worried about how her husband was handling quarantine and the inequitable treatment of their Black community. Another woman drove to the grocery store daily, mostly to escape from her house, coming home exhausted from the anxiety of being in the world, and falling asleep dreaming of the sumptuous meal she'd make. A Black man contemplated the mask he has been forced to wear all his life.

And then George Floyd's murder united so many of us in a grief that certainly was not new. His final words, "I can't breathe," sparked a connection that took us out of our dark COVID-19 fugue state. It had us asking a vast, overwhelming question that became the pumping heart of this book: **What Now?**

The privilege and reward of putting together this Lovely Monster was that it allowed me to unite for a common good with ninety-one authors (sixty-nine in the print book and another twenty-two in the e-book and audio editions) from diverse cultures and backgrounds. This book has developed a soul thanks to every one of them. She holds our collective pain and our dreams, and I hope she offers you what she has given me: a renewed sense of possibilities. In telling our stories, we hope to enable you to tell your story. That's the sweet spot of connections, where the healing happens.

ALONE TOGETHER

LOVE, GRIEF, AND COMFORT IN THE TIME OF COVID-19

PART ONE: WHAT NOW?

IN CONVERSATION WITH
KWAME ALEXANDER

"In order to feel like you're heard, you need to say something."

Kwame Alexander has a gift for "making our blues beautiful," as he has demonstrated time and again on National Public Radio's "Morning Edition," crowd-sourcing lines of verse contributed by upwards of one thousand listeners nationwide to create one emotionally charged poem. During this crisis of health, economy, and democracy in the U.S., Alexander has provided a space for our country to unite through the beauty of our words, a means to express shared grief and fear, to hope for better days. Here's more from NPR's poet-in-residence about the power of sharing our stories:

Jennifer Haupt: All of our lives, our stories, are changing during the pandemic lockdown. What's the new normal for your family?

Kwame Alexander: I have an eleven-year-old at home and I spend a great deal of my time trying to keep her engaged with life. During the past forty days or so, my daughter and I have played softball in front of our flat, we've played catch, we've hula-hooped, we've thrown Frisbees, we just got a skateboard—I'm teaching her how to use it. We're doing these things we didn't have time for in the past because we were so busy with our lives.

What's the new normal now? I'm finding that we're going back to some of the things that we used to do growing up and my kid is enjoying it! That's encouraging and exciting for me as a parent. It's show-ing me how to have a balance between technology and this visceral, touchy—I don't even know what you call it, but it's how I grew up. These shared experiences are bringing us closer together, and I think that's one of the gifts of this time, that we're going to develop some new *old* ways of interacting with each other.

JH: Our kids are actually getting sick of technology. Who knew that could happen? I'm wondering, how is this time going to change the way we teach our children and might there be some positive outcomes?

KA: How are we going to make our blues beautiful? It's all about perspective. The same basic ideas will still matter—getting our kids to not just read, but to want to read; teaching them not just to write, but to want to write. Creating opportunities for our kids to learn how to think. All of that will remain the same. What's going to matter now is, how are we as educators going to use our creativity to innovate, to adapt, in this new way of learning?

Part of that involves technology: bringing more guest speakers into the classroom using Zoom is one example. But part of the cre-ativity has nothing to do with technology. There's a teacher in Lexing-ton County, South Carolina, her name is Melanie Thornton, and she teaches in a community where a lot of her students don't have Wi-Fi. So what does she do during the lockdown? She gets into her golf cart and drives around the neighborhood, reading aloud. She stops at each student's house and reads a picture book.

JH: Encouraging children to tell their stories is a big part of what you do. What's the power of telling one's story?

KA: Everybody wants to feel like they're heard. In order to feel like you're heard, you need to say something. Telling our stories gives us a voice. It also lifts our voices; it allows us to sing it out into the world. That makes us feel confident, that makes us feel better, that makes us understand ourselves even better.

It's almost like we're communicating with ourselves. We're saying, "Hey, this is who you are. This is what you've been through; this is where you're going." The ancient Egyptians said, "So it is written, so it shall be." I am declaring it. Now, when I put my story out into the world and someone else reads it, responds to it, connects with it—ah, now I feel like I matter to the world. I am a part of some place bigger than me. I think that is crucial, especially during times of intense and difficult change.

JH: The beauty of books, sharing our stories, for both the author and readers, is incredible. It's a superpower of connection.

KA: Words and books show us that we're all one, you know? Like, I can read *Night* by Elie Wiesel and know that I have no direct connection to having been in a concentration camp, yet I feel it. I understand its weight and heaviness, its evil and terror, the author's fight and survival—I understand all that. Books, literature, and language allow us to understand that we are more similar than we are different.

JH: No matter what background we come from or how much money we have, everyone is affected by the pandemic. I'm hoping that connection of fighting a common enemy shifts the conversations from "others" being the enemies to the disease being the enemy we're all fighting.

KA: That has been my hope for a very long time, that we can be united by something bigger than all of our differences. And it may take some reeducating, for sure. My lifelong purpose is to help young people, because I think maybe the adults have screwed up a little bit too much. I don't know if there's any hope for us, but I want to help children imagine a better world. A big part of that is helping them tell their stories of the past, the present, and the future.

JH: How important is it that we keep listening to each other? How do we use our stories, our understanding to keep the momentum of social activism going?

KA: I tell my eleven-year-old she can learn far more by listening than talking. When we read, we are listening to the writer offering us a glimpse of the world that we may not see by ourselves. When we hear music, we are listening to the rhythms and sounds that make us feel something that we weren't feeling before. Listening is what allows us to learn. Something. Anything. Everything. And, it is that learning that we bring to our daily lives which opens up a world of possibility, about who we can be, how we can be, and what ought to be. And, isn't that where our stories come from?

KWAME ALEXANDER is the Innovator-in-Residence at the American School of London, and the *New York Times* bestselling author of thirty-four books, including the Newbery Medal-winning middle grade novel, *The Crossover*. As the Founding Editor of Versify, an imprint of Houghton Mifflin Harcourt, he aims to change the world, one word at a time.

THE NEW OLD VOCABULARY

By Faith Adiele

WEEK 1: SHELTER

As introverts, you're content to shelter in place. You move quiet and smiling through the house. Pass the time watching Netflix and Instagram DJs (you), CNN and WhatsApp conspiracy videos (him). Self-soothe by cooking from the *Times* (you) or consuming chips and matzo and grits and dollar-store cookies (him). You try not to judge. Midweek he makes a run for the border, driving seven hours to So-Cal and crossing on foot into Tijuana to get crowns installed. As he's leaving the dentist, the U.S. and Mexico announce border closures. *I'm driving straight back!* he texts. *Okay,* you reply, distracted by the clowder of cats battling across the street (though they're feral, so technically it's a destruction of cats). *But not without TP and mezcal!*

On your birthday, a cruise ship sails under Golden Gate Bridge to dock in Oakland, 5.2 miles from your house. Twenty-one people aboard (nineteen of them crew members) test positive for coronavirus. After a week it relocates to the Black neighborhood of Hunters Point, offloading one million gallons of raw sewage.

WEEK 2: ISOLATE

As members of #ShelterPrivilege, you feel pressure to win at #QuarantineLife. To learn a foreign language. To make virtual visits to museum collections you didn't wanna see in real life. To take walks and post footage of inspiring vistas. To attend nightly poetry readings and morning yoga. To be crafting, always crafting. To raise sourdough pets, despite the fact that, after the initial panic-shopping that cleared stores of eggs, egg substitute, rice and breadstuffs, the Bay Area abounds with bread. You hear your husband bragging on the phone about how well he's eating, how lucky he is that his wife bakes. If only he'd married sooner, by God, he'd be rich by now!

Around the world, domestic battery rates soar as stay-at-home orders are implemented, layoffs increase, and women and children are trapped with men with histories of domestic violence.

WEEK 3: WASH

Black Brunch Club moves online, folks giddy to see capitalism on hold. "Clearly the old system wasn't working," they crow. "It collapsed so quickly and completely!" You burst into tears. Until now, you've been doing fine. Hunched over your laptop, you drip tears onto your keyboard condom, sniffles drowned out by a dreadlocked guy who's cooking & chewing & pouring bleach into spray bottles, all on UN-MUTE. Speaking of fools, in a giant tragicomedy of errors, your literary agent *just* sent out the manuscript you've been tinkering with for years. Nobody in New York is buying. You're not ready for a new world order. You've worked too hard at the old one. You need a book contract and tenure. Then the revolution. Besides, you can't imagine any national or global crisis benefitting Black & Brown folks in the end.

A former student, a South Asian physician, says he'll be treating coronavirus patients. What narrative should I document? he asks. Ours, you reply. Eventually he follows Doctors Without Borders to the Navajo Na-

tion, penning a poem about leaving his kids: "Tears fall/big drops against their full brown cheeks."

WEEK 4: ENFORCEMENT

After weeks huddled in bed watching CNN like a car crash, your husband decides to Go Out. The two of you square off in the kitchen, arms akimbo. He hasn't worked in months; someone has to pay the mortgage. He thinks you're afraid to go out, but you simply don't have time to mask up and stand in line to buy groceries or #SaveThePost-Office. In the beginning you patronized ethnic eateries & food trucks & indie bookstores you wanted to support, but now there's no time. Besides, delivery people need work. You're not sure where to set your Worry-o-meter—on telling an African man he can't work, or on him taking his high-risk ass outside. He was fifty-seven when you wed and is now sixty-plus. The instant you exchanged vows, you started worrying about his mortality. Fortunately, he's a germophobe. "I'd never sleep around in regular times," he rationalizes, spritzing groceries, "or break social distancing now!" He's downright giddy at permission to go bleach-crazy, an African habit you used to fight about.

Your iPhones are linked, so you self-soothe by watching waves pulse from the blue dot that's him in line at Trader Joe's, at The Home Depot, at Dollar Tree. Errands take forever, partly due to social distancing measures, partly because everything's new to him: *What's chutney and where do you find it? When you say milk, do you mean nonfat, two percent, whole, buttermilk, lactose-free, organic, chocolate, powdered, tinned? Oh. What's a shallot?* You learn to keep your phone charged. "Our neighborhood is so poor no one can afford to stock up," he marvels upon his return, hours later. "I found everything!" One day you forget to track him, and he returns with a haircut. Eyes narrowed over the mask, he dares you to say something.

Guns and tasers drawn, Oakland police handcuff two Black men delivering food and supplies to homeless communities. NYPD starts enforcing social-distancing rules; Blacks and Hispanics comprise 81.6 percent of summons and 92 percent of arrests.

WEEK 5: EXPOSURE

A Taiwanese American Muslim friend asks you to cohost an online session for writers of color. You decline. You're always doing things for free, for so-called "exposure." "Easy things" that shouldn't take time, but, let's face it, you're gonna obsess, prepare, rewrite, redesign. It's a sickness. Your friend says, "Speaking of sickness, New York is really suffering, not like California." She grins, finger hovering over SEND until you nod. The next day thirty shiny faces pop on your screen like a brown Brady Bunch. She monitors the virtual door, welcoming folks by name, patrolling for racist Zoombombers, which is now apparently a thing. You're in charge of the touchy-feely stuff. You call on folks to share two minutes each. They come, week after week, word of mouth growing the group to fifty-plus. Literary acquaintances, friends from other lives and cities, strangers from as far away as the Philippines. You yourself are blocked, so you marvel at the way this rainbow Hollywood Squares takes your heart apart and puts it back together in two-minute increments.

Across the country, anti-Asian harassment increases, reminiscent of the medical scapegoating that occurred just across the bridge in the 1870s, when

San Francisco officials blamed smallpox and bubonic plague outbreaks on Chinatown's "foul and disgusting vapors."

WEEK 6: BOUNDARIES

You spend twelve hours a day Zooming, Google-Hangouting, FaceTiming. Your Wi-Fi isn't great. You never quite seem to be heard. The people who seem not to hear you most are white men and older white women. One Karen allows you a single sentence then cuts you off. Again. "That's it!" you shriek, pounding the red LEAVE MEETING button as it were a slammable door. Two days later you find yourself muting another Karen as she drones on about something you'd advised her not to ask the Black guest speaker. Afterward you call your mom: "The Karens will kill me before the 'rona does!" you rage. "Ugh," your white mother groans, "my people." When Black Twitter declares the collective noun for a group of Karens is a "privilege," you're healed.

The Navajo Nation registers the highest per capita rate of COVID-19 in the country, higher than New York. It's the latest in five hundred years of "epidemiological invasions," which, combined with colonial practices, wiped out 70 to 90 percent of Native populations by the early twentieth century.

WEEK 7: AT-RISK

It becomes clear that those who are dying are Black & Brown. Your people have always been both essential & expendable. Both crap workers (farm workers, food servers, delivery people, garbage picker-uppers) and specialists (nurses, home healthcare providers, lab techs, #NigerianDoctors). The Bay Area's highest rates of infection and death are in your neighborhood of poor Blacks & Latinos. The Black female mayor of white San Francisco takes action; the white female mayor of Black Oakland hides out. Neighbors on Nextdoor accuse you of making everything about race. *Yes*, you respond, *exactly*.

But you're privileged. Privileged to have a job that allows you to work online twelve hours a day. Privileged to live in The Bay with its sunny weather & food delivery & farmers' markets & governor who knows how to lead & read. And though armed, unmasked Californians, draped in camo, patrol the countryside, whining about oppression, at least you're not in a state full of them, the state of white privilege.

In Chicago alone, Blacks account for 72 percent of virus related fatalities. "Those numbers take your breath away, they really do," says Mayor Lightfoot. Six hours away, in Minneapolis, a policeman will kneel on a Black man's neck as he begs, #ICantBreathe.

WEEK 8: RESISTANCE

Someone at Black Brunch muses, "Is this germ warfare or Mother Nature trying to rid herself of the human virus?" Weeks later, #HumansAreTheVirus becomes a hashtag, accompanied by photos of animals invading cities and a giant rubber ducky sailing the Thames. This suits you just fine. CNN may be playing on an endless loop upstairs, but the only pandemic news you want are accounts of bears living it up in Yosemite. Dolphins frolicking in blue Venetian canals. Goats clip-clopping through financial districts. That lone coyote prowling San Francisco like a Bizarro-World version of the old ad with the fake Native American and his glycerin tear.

The rare occasion you drag yourself outside, your neighborhood is barren, no more cats prowling the creek bed. Your neighborhood is transitional, trucks idling before your house in broad daylight, offloading mattresses & clothes & broken furniture & toys into the narrow park. You rush outside, hoping to shame these un-neighbors, but even if they looked up, they wouldn't see the scowl behind your mask anyway. At night you toss in bed, feverish, listening for feline yowls, tracking the shallow breathing of the man beside you. There are fewer gunshots, fewer squealing tires, fewer 'copters overhead. How did an entire clowder (or destruction) vanish? How will your people manage to resist, yet again?

Credits:
Marsh, Julia, et al., "Blacks, Hispanics Make up Most of NYPD Social-Distancing Summonses, Arrests," *New York Post*, May 8, 2020.
Okorafor, Nnedi. "Five Things COVID-19 Has Taught Me about Life," *The Lagos Review*, April 19, 2020.
Rios, Desiree. "Black Americans Face Alarming Rates of Coronavirus Infection in Some States," *New York Times*, Apr 7, 2020.
Shamasunder, Sriram. "Going into the Hospital: COVID 19 (Poem)," *Daily Good*, May 8, 2020.
Smithers, Gregory D. "COVID-19 Has Been Brutal in Indian Country—Just Like Past Epidemics Were," *Washington Post*, May 20, 2020.
Zhou, Li. "How the Coronavirus Is Surfacing America's Deep-Seated Anti-Asian Biases," *Vox*, Apr 21, 2020.

FAITH ADIELE is the author of two memoirs—*Meeting Faith*, which won the PEN Open Book Award, and *The Nigerian-Nordic Girl's Guide to Lady Problems*. She lives in Oakland, California, where she is the founder of African Book Club and VONA Travel, the nation's first workshop for travel writers of color.

VIGILANCE AND SURRENDER

By Andre Dubus III

It is a sort of elation, a razored clarity, and it magnifies every car on the road so that I see the minute scratches on their hoods, the caked mud in their wheel wells; it makes every masked woman or man in the grocery store nearly four-dimensional, the hairs of their ears visible though I might be six feet away or more; it makes each traffic light hanging over the street as close as if I am holding it in both hands, flakes of rust on either side of it, the glass lenses pointed at my vigilant self, who has always known the world would face a calamity like this, who has been waiting for it really. For since I was very young, I have been expecting disaster everywhere and at all times.

I'm driving south on 495, the April sun high overhead. My mask hangs loosely beneath my chin. It is a much-needed N95 mask that I pulled from the pocket of my leather carpenter's belt in the basement. I bought this mask months ago to protect my lungs from sawdust when I was building my family a dining room table that can seat as many as twenty-four people. I did this in our house in the woods forty miles north of Boston, a house I was so lucky to have built with my own hands with my only brother, fifteen years ago. He designed it, and then he and I and a small crew spent nearly three years making those drawings real. After cutting down trees and blasting into a hill of rock, we built the first floor for my wife Fontaine's aging parents and then the three floors above were to hold us and our three children, who were then twelve, ten, and eight.

When we were finally able to move in to our new home-made

15

house on a cold sunny March afternoon, I was forty-five years old and had never lived anywhere without a landlord. Late one of those first nights, lying in bed next to Fontaine who was asleep, I counted the rented houses and apartments I'd grown up in and lived in as a young man. The number was twenty-five.

There are very few cars on this highway, though it is late afternoon on a weekday, the usual time for commuters to head home. I take the Byfield exit, pull over, and call my brother-in-law on my flip phone. He is a retired school teacher in his early seventies, one of the kindest men I know, and I'm calling him to tell him that I'm five minutes away, that I was able to buy all the groceries on his list except for the antiseptic hand wipes, which are gone, as is all the toilet paper on the store's shelves, and the flour and the pasta and the bottled water. I am shopping for my brother-in-law because he and his wife, a woman also in her seventies, have the virus.

They believe that she probably contracted it where she works as a nurse in a home for the elderly. Her symptoms came before his did. She lost her senses of smell and taste, and then she started throwing up and couldn't stop, and my brother-in-law drove her to the hospital where they put her on an IV for a while before sending her home. When her test came back positive, the town's Board of Health called and told them to stay in their house for weeks.

The first few years living in our lovely home with all of its windows and natural light, its wide-open downstairs where we hosted parties for friends and family all year long, inviting my in-laws up to join us, this structure of wood and glass where our kids felt safe and loved, I'd lie in bed late at night, unable to sleep, waiting for any rolling crunch of tires out in our gravel driveway to be a car load of men come to beat me to death. Beside my bed leaned a baseball bat I was prepared to use, but most nights, instead of expecting the kind of street trouble I'd known as a kid, I feared it was the landlord coming for the rent I did not have. I'd have to tell myself that I owned this house, no one else, except for the bank from whom I'd had to borrow, and so now I worried about them coming to take everything, even though I paid my bills, even though I wrote and published books that sold well, even though I was a university professor, even though my wife now owned a dance studio downtown.

Such abundance, and I was used to none of it. I had grown up in poverty, the son of a single mother in half-dead mill towns where I had had a violent youth, one I've written about elsewhere and won't go into here, but the thing you should know is that things going consistently well for me has been like living in a foreign country, one where I'm still trying to learn the language.

My brother-in-law thanks me and tells me he'll leave the garage door open. He asks if I'm sure I don't need any help with the groceries. I tell him no, that I want to be a mile down the road before he even steps into that garage. We both laugh and then he starts to cough, and I hang up.

Twenty years ago, my third published book became a bestseller and made me and my young family a lot of money. I was forty and had been writing daily since I was twenty-two. To support my writing habit in my twenties, I worked as a construction laborer, a bartender, and a half-way house counselor. In my thirties, after publishing my first two books, I taught as an adjunct creative writing professor at various colleges in Boston, but I made most of my living as a self-employed carpenter. Until the wild success of my third book, I'd never had more than three hundred dollars in the bank and now I had so much more than that, I could not get rid of it fast enough.

I treated friends and family to trips and ballgames and boat rides. I bought my mother—a woman who never owned anything but used cars with well over 150,000 miles on them—a brand-new pickup truck. I'd lend friends thousands of dollars with them barely even asking for it. And as I was doing all this, I seemed to be operating under a dual awareness of myself: half of me took joy in the good times I was finally able to spark and spread around, but the other half could see that I would not feel like myself again until I was broke. Those days, I often felt like I was walking on a boat drifting through high seas.

When I pull into my brother-in-law's driveway, the late afternoon sun is shining on his new tool shed, on his well-tended lawn and flower garden, on the clapboards of this new home he and his wife built for their retirement. I turn my truck around so that it's pointing back to the road, then I pull on my mask and a fresh pair of latex gloves, leave my engine running, and in two trips carry a dozen bags of groceries into my brother-in-law's garage. As I climb back behind the wheel, he comes out on the front porch in his mask and thanks me, waving as I drive away.

In the back seat of my truck are also my brother's groceries, and in the front are groceries for my mother and my mother-in-law, who is nearly ninety-nine. We are particularly worried about her catching this thing, this widow of nearly eleven years who still does all her own cleaning and cooking, who drives her sporty leased Toyota to the gym twice a week, who goes to church on Sundays and helps my wife at the dance studio on Friday mornings when she enters into the ledger all the people who have shown up for the Zumba class. We have been living quite happily together for fifteen years, and she's become one of my best friends.

When I show up at her door with her groceries, wearing my mask and a new pair of gloves, she greets me from only two or three feet away, and I have to tell her to go to the other side of the room. "Oh," she says, "I keep forgetting." She asks for my receipt and insists on paying me back in cash for her groceries before I even finish unpacking them. As I do, I know that she does not forget about the virus because daily she is moved to tears by all the dying she sees on the news. "Why?" she'll ask me. "Why has this *happened*?"

I ask her to leave the money on her kitchen table and then please step into the hallway before I retrieve it. She thanks me in Greek, and says, "Sagapo," I love you, and I say it back.

Then I'm in my truck again, driving along the Merrimack River, the late-day sun glinting off its swirling surface. I pass a house with signs on the lawn thanking our doctors and nurses and essential workers, and I think how my younger brother suffers from diabetes and three kinds of cancer, how his doctor says he has the immune system of an AIDS patient. At my brother's apartment, I leave my truck engine running, pull on my mask and new gloves, then leave his groceries on his porch. As I put my truck in gear, his eighteen-year-old daughter Nina comes out and blows me a kiss before gathering up the bags and disappearing inside.

If I had not been a father and a husband, I believe I would have blown all that money twenty years ago. But Fontaine made it clear that it was time we had a home of our own, something other than the dark, cramped half-house we'd been renting for the past eleven years, our three young children sharing the same room. But these were largely the conditions in which I was raised, and so it took a while for me to imagine something different, to imagine that we might actually build something, that we might have a home of our own.

My next stop is my mother's place, just a mile or so down the road from my brother's. She is eighty-one and last year had triple bypass surgery, though she still works part-time as an addictions counselor. She lives alone on the first floor of a house she owns, and when I pull up to my mother's I see that her car is in the driveway. I'm relieved because I fear she leaves the house more frequently than she should.

I park on a side street, pull on my mask and a fresh pair of gloves, and call her on the phone so that she'll bring out to the porch her bags of trash and recycling. She does this, then waits inside until I've carried them out to the barrels in the driveway. I set her bags of groceries on the narrow porch and then wait on the sidewalk for her to come back outside. We chat briefly from twenty feet away. My lovely mother's hair is white, and it pains me that I cannot hug her, this woman who raised me and my three siblings largely alone, in one rented house or apartment after another, this woman whom we all worry about more than ever before. She thanks me, then says, "You're the family Sherpa."

And as I wave at my mother and drive away, I picture those Himalayan men, paid to haul climbers' food and supplies up steep mountains. It is an image that seems to ripple through me, for throughout this strange, hard time I've been thinking a lot about the words *love* and *family* and *friends* and *community*, and I think about our three children, who not so long ago were moving with us into our new homemade house in the woods and now they are twenty-seven, twenty-four, and twenty-three, all living full lives elsewhere, though the oldest two have come home for a while, and they do not like me being the one to shop for others. They tell me that I'm old and that I could die and I see the same fear in their faces that I've held for so long in the depths of my own heart. But how can I tell them that I feel most at home when things are perilous? That all that is wonderful in this world is frighteningly temporary and so when abundance of any kind comes, we must celebrate it, for what has saved me, what has asked me to open myself and trust in something larger, is my love for them and for their mother, for my larger family and many friends, and I want to hug my children and tell them that it's okay, but we cannot hug, can we?

And so we have to show our love in other ways. We have to climb the mountains rising up before us, food strapped to our backs, our faces covered with masks as we say, "Stay safe. Stay healthy." Don't leave. Ever.

National Book Award Finalist ANDRE DUBUS III is the author of seven books, most recently his 2018 novel, *Gone So Long.* He lives in Newbury, Massachusetts, with his wife and three children.

AT TIMES LIKE THIS
(FOR MAYA ANGELOU)

By Nikki Giovanni

At times like this
We measure our words
Because we are
Measuring a life

A friend was not
Lost nor did she
Transition she
Died

We recognize a good
Life was lead a
Generous heart
Ceases to beat
A hearty laugh will
No longer be
Heard

We measure not
The depth
But the width
Of compassion
And passion
And dreams

We place our love
Gently
On the flowers
  That cover her
Under the clouds
  That embrace her
Into the Earth
  That owns her
And now
  Reclaims her

We will miss her
Spirit Her demands
Her hopes for us
And therefore Herself
At times like this
We are sad
We gather
We comfort
Each other
Yet still
At times like this
We
Properly
Cry

NIKKI GIOVANNI is a celebrated poet, writer, and speaker. She is a University Distinguished Professor at Virginia Tech.

GHOST TOWN

By Scott James

I wasn't sure what to expect as we drove onto the Stanford campus. The university had been shuttered for weeks, with students sent home and classes moved online as California sheltered in place.

But not everyone could go home.

For some, home was not a safe haven from the pandemic—the virus raged in their countries and borders were sealed. Others came from poverty or housing instability where remote learning was impossible. And there were students from nations embattled with the Trump administration, for whom going back meant they'd never return.

Those left behind were scattered across campus, isolated in dorm rooms or off-campus housing. They could not shelter with loved ones, but we could make a gesture of home.

My husband, Jerry, teaches computer science at Stanford, and when his class went virtual it also became enormous. It was not unusual for a lecturer to have one hundred fifty students or more in a quarter, but in the switch to online learning, the university eliminated grades and made classes pass/fail. Suddenly the stakes seemed lower for a notoriously demanding course, and enrollment for Jerry's class surged to more than five hundred.

With so many students, it was inevitable that Jerry would have at least some of the left-behinds. Eventually he determined that fifteen of his students were stuck at school.

In twenty-four years of teaching, Jerry had never been in a situation where he would not meet any of his students. One day, between coding assignments and Zoom office hours, he computed a solution: banana bread.

He decided to bake homemade banana bread and deliver the loaves to the stranded. They'd share a few moments of socially distanced face time, and in a small way he'd close some of the chasm inflicted by the virus.

As we drove through the maze of narrow tree-strewn roads to our first stop, handfuls of joggers, walkers, and cyclists peppered the school's paths. Among them were small children, some on tricycles.

"That's a sophomore," Jerry joked as we passed a toddler.

I'd forgotten that faculty, graduate students, and their families lived here too. When they were ordered home, they stayed.

In addition to the banana bread, we brought a goodwill ambassador, our lively red-haired Boston terrier, Doris. She wagged her nubby tail as we parked. Across the lot, five students stood near the school's auditorium, meeting each other for the first time, six feet apart, some in masks, some not.

That's when I saw something I'd missed for a long time.

Smiles.

———

Jerry and I had been sheltering in place thirty miles north in San Francisco, in our home in the city's famed Castro neighborhood. When the lockdown came, our once-busy streets became a ghost town.

Closed businesses covered their windows in plywood, causing an outcry by some local politicians and residents who worried about the disturbing message of such visual blight. The precautions, however, were wise. Soon those who did not secure their stores discovered their windows smashed.

Vacated stores weren't the only targets. The local Walgreens was a lifeline for the community, and though it remained open twenty-four hours a day for medicine and food, it too was forced to board its windows.

Neighbors sealed their shades. Only traces revealed life behind darkly secured edifices, like children's chalk rainbows on sidewalks, or anxious postings on hyper-local websites like Nextdoor.

Siege mentality was further fueled by a phone app called Citizen, which turns police and fire scanner traffic into instant alerts. No one needed to peek out windows to determine why sirens blared—the news came to you instantly inside your bunker.

With streets abandoned, those who remained outside were those who were already there—the unhoused, addicted, and mentally ill. The city's failure to intercede over the course of plentiful years was now on disturbing display. Open-air needle drug use, defecation, and despair confronted those who ventured from their homes. Filthy encampments crowded sidewalks, their existence an act of "compassion," some city leaders argued. After all, homeless shelters were petri dishes for the spread of disease.

None of this was new. The pandemic just made it worse, or at least more visible. San Francisco, and especially the Castro, had been on a downward spiral for years. Dozens of businesses around us had recently folded—many due to the overall decline of brick and mortar retail, but a significant number of others felt unsafe or were unwilling to absorb the costs and hassles of doing business here, in a neighborhood renowned as a birthplace of the gay rights movement, and one of the few remaining so-called gayborhoods in the United States.

People will argue over how it happened, but a loss in social norms had already taken a heavy toll on the Castro. Basic tenets of acceptable, even criminal, behavior were no longer agreed upon.

Several departing businesses pointed to a change in laws a few years ago that, in essence, decriminalized many crimes. It may have been a well-intentioned effort to reform the criminal justice system, but in practice, in San Francisco, it meant that unless a crime exceeded an extreme threshold, a person would not be prosecuted or held accountable. Stores could be robbed, and staff threatened with violence, and there were be few, if any, consequences. The Castro felt lawless to some business owners, and they gave up.

I'd written about the city's decline in my newspaper work. It wasn't more spotlight that was needed, but solutions. Viable answers were in short supply, and leaders appeared inept. A recent FBI investigation, arrests, and a growing City Hall corruption scandal promised to shed some light on why the city was so mismanaged.

Then came COVID 19.

The Castro now sometimes looked apocalyptic—mentally disturbed people, some covered in feces, wandered and shouted at invisible demons. These were human beings, not fictional zombies. Still, officials didn't help.

The pandemic loosened the city's social fabric in other ways too. With so few on the road, and lax enforcement, drivers largely stopped using turn signals and ceased obeying other traffic rules. More than once, walking Doris, we'd been missed by inches as cars barreled through red lights or stop signs.

Other eroding norms were more curious than dangerous. Men in the neighborhood stopped wearing underwear with sweatpants or gym shorts, leaving little to the imagination.

"Maybe they've run out of clean undies," a friend said. She reasoned that perhaps those going commando couldn't access laundry during the shutdown.

Only when I noticed others doing errands in their pajamas did I realize that the lack of underwear was because people were going outside wearing the clothes they'd just slept in. It wasn't exhibitionism. Dressing had become as blurry as the days of the week.

By decree, our faces became armored with masks. When people approached it was impossible to determine if they were happy or threatening.

Then one Saturday night, the Castro's troubles came to our home.

A disturbed man in his thirties, his face wildly distorted by screams, climbed to the top deck of our building and threatened to jump and kill himself. Six police officers brandishing rifles and pistols stormed through our home, apprehended the man, then dragged him in handcuffs through our bedroom and out to an ambulance.

"You're hurting me!" the man yelled.

Officers never bothered to ask our names for a report. The incident wasn't even significant enough to be posted on that Citizen phone app.

———

So when we arrived at Stanford to deliver banana bread, those smiles from students were welcome.

At home, everything we loved about the Castro—the people, the places, the culture—felt dangerous. On campus, we were suddenly transported to a realm of hope and possibility. Students represent the future, and they seemed grateful for the token of a homemade goodie.

Doris sealed the deal with little terrier kisses for everyone.

"You made my day," said one young woman as she received her bread before wandering back alone to her dorm. "Actually, you made my week!"

Jerry and I remained wrapped up tight for our campus visit, never removing our gloves and masks. We still had on our city armor.

Underneath, though, we smiled.

Scott James is the author of *Trial by Fire: A Devastating Tragedy, 100 Lives Lost, and a 15-Year Search for Truth*. Since 2009 he has been a frequent contributor to the *New York Times,* and he's been honored with three Emmy Awards for his work in television news.

FEEDING MY HEART AND SOUL

By Andrea King Collier

I am spending a fortune on groceries. I am spending so much money that when anybody asks me casually just how much, I lowball it. Each week I spend triple what I did pre-virus, and still feel like I do not have enough.

But food's not the only reason I go to the grocery store: in the age of stay-at-home orders and lockdowns, this is the only way I get out of the house. My daily grocery runs, armed with my mask, wipes, and hand sanitizer, have replaced going to the bookstore, having lunch with friends, and visiting my grandchildren. It's been like this for the past ten weeks, since early March.

Sometimes I go when I don't even need anything—I just sit in the parking lot, listening to NPR, until I am tired and go home. My trips feel like I am running from 'rona. But lately, grocery shopping also connects me with a comfort around food I have had since childhood, and it anchors me in the face of the other pandemic that has come to a head with the murder of George Floyd but has been a virus growing in our country for many years: hate and racism.

When I was little, I went to the grocery store almost every day with my grandfather. I never asked why we did this, because I didn't care. I just knew that it was time with him. They call these teachable moments now. He showed me how to pick out tomatoes that were going to be rich and juicy, how to tell when a chicken was too big and would be tough, and how to check the dates on the dairy products. And so much more.

Once, in the A&P, a white woman whose toddler was perched in the front seat of her cart turned and called us niggers to our faces—for no apparent reason—and then stormed away. It was startling, because our little shopping trips had always been uneventful. I had never been called that before, and I wondered how my grandpa managed to contain himself. He didn't even stop adding rice, beans, and onions to the cart.

A few aisles later, we saw the same woman. She was screaming and crying because the toddler was choking on something. Everybody stood around fretting, but nobody was doing anything.

My grandfather, who knew how to fix everything, held out his hands and told the lady to give the baby to him. He was the only thing standing between her and a dead child, so she handed the little girl over. He held the toddler horizontally, her stomach facing the floor, and gave her a swift slap her on her back, dislodging a piece of candy from her throat. Then he handed her back. The mother just stood there, mouth open The bystanders applauded. And when we went to pay for the groceries, the store manager said, "They are on us."

In the parking lot, I asked my grandfather why he helped that woman who hadn't even bothered to thank him. "Because that's what good people do when they can," he said. "We look out for each other."

Now, in month three of the COVID-19 pandemic, the lockdown is lifting around the country but there's also a curfew triggered by protests in many cities with armed police in the streets. I often think about my trips to the A&P with my grandfather, as I put on my unattractive protective masks every damn day. I nod to others who wear masks; maybe they can't stay home either.

I must admit that this cooking and food-shopping thing is a first-world, privileged problem in a country where thousands of people get this virus every day and where the economy has taken a nosedive. As I see stories on the thousands of families that line up at the food banks, it does trigger my fears of scarcity. I am aware that there are people who are worried not about cooking, but about having anything to eat at all. And yet this does not stop me. The shame does not stop me. It's the one thing I have control over right now.

Now, I am a food warrior in the stores, buying way too much of the food that makes my heart sing. I go get many of the foods that my grandfather and I used to shop for all those years ago. I regularly buy stone-ground grits, dried black-eyed peas, corn on the cob, and bell peppers. I always come back home with catfish, because that was one of our favorites. Who knew that old-school shopping would be an act of resistance against a very dangerous virus, but also an act that reminds me of my Black family pride and traditions?

I usually come home so exhausted that I don't have the energy to cook right away. I take a nap, dreaming up fabulous meals, like macaroni and cheese, baked ham and red gravy, potato salad just the way my grandma used to make it.

ANDREA KING COLLIER is a multimedia journalist, essayist, and author based in Lansing, Michigan. She is the author of *Still with Me . . . A Daughter's Journey of Love and Loss*, and *The Black Woman's Guide to Black Men's Health*.

SHEDDING

By Gayle Brandeis

The virus sheds
and sheds
       us
of illusion—
of safety,
of vanity,
of separateness.

The virus sheds
and sheds
      light
on inequity
on injustice
on our interdependence

The virus sheds
and we shed
       tears
          shed
            light
for one another,
offering compassion
and commiseration,
material help
and ethereal hope

The virus sheds
and we shed
      what doesn't
         serve us
so we can focus
on what matters

GAYLE BRANDEIS is the author, most recently, of the memoir *The Art of Misdiagnosis*, and the novel in poems *Many Restless Concerns*.

SIT THE HELL DOWN

By Dinty W. Moore

After more than thirty-three years of teaching writing to college students, the unexpected happened. I found myself starting to lose steam, began searching for an expiration date. Nothing had changed, really: the students were great, the job was a privilege. But I grew increasingly tired of hearing myself talk. And when I walked by the classrooms of younger teachers, I sensed an energy that my own classes no longer had.

So I announced that spring 2020 would be my final semester, and as my last day in the classroom neared, I let myself dream. I imagined my retirement as a bursting forth, a late-stage adventure, a time to travel, to commence with goals long put off by faculty meetings and marking student papers.

Maybe it will be, someday.

Right now, though, well into our pandemic social-distancing protocol, my retirement looks like this:

Stay the hell home. Sit the hell down. Stare out the window. Watch for the mail. Spy on the neighbors out of sheer boredom. If the sun is warm enough, wander my sixteen-by-sixteen-foot backyard until I can name every blade of grass and identify every loose bit of brick on the retaining wall.

Over the years, I've watched as elderly neighbors lived this sort of restricted life and thought, "Not me, no way, no chance." But whoever is in charge of this world has their own sense of humor.

Postponed. Suspended. That's how it all feels. I'm not fully out of my old life but neither am I quite in my new life. I feel like a bug, sealed in amber but wide awake.

Buddhist teachers have been urging us for many years now to live in the present moment, and now that we can, it turns out to be very, very difficult. This is not the moment we chose. This is not a moment sparkling with possibility. Not a sunrise on a mountain. The moment, to be honest—if you are lucky enough to be healthy, and not fighting the virus on the front lines—is rather dull.

As retirement neared, I often assured my friends (and myself), "Oh, I'll be busy. It's not as if I'm going to just sit in my easy chair all day, staring at the wall." Now I sit in my easy chair and can't stop thinking of my favorite John Lennon quote, "Life is what happens to you while you're busy making other plans."

My plan for today is to make dinner.

Retirement doesn't feel so different. Just the new normal.

Lots of people are suspended in amber right now.

But at least I retired by choice. There's a blessing I have to count.

I'm still here. That's another blessing.

And that wall?

I'm staring at the wall, more than I ever planned, but also noticing that when the afternoon sun streams through the living room window, it takes on beautiful shadows.

DINTY W. MOORE is the author of numerous books of nonfiction, including the forthcoming *To Hell with It: Of Sin and Sex, Chicken Wings, and Dante's Entirely Ridiculous, Needlessly Guilt-Inducing Inferno*. He lives in Athens, Ohio.

BOOKS ON PAUSE

By Kevin Sampsell

Maybe I jinxed it. In early March, I said to a fellow bookseller at Powell's: "It would be weird if it got so bad that we had to close the store and only do online orders."

My comment came in the shooting-the-shit spirit of a retail work-day. At the time, it seemed an outrageous mental picture, even though growing concerns about the coronavirus were causing some customers to wear masks and gloves and many authors to cancel their events at the store. Just six days later, on March 15, our store, the largest new and used bookstore in the world and a Portland institution for nearly fifty years, closed its doors in viral surrender. The first game plan was to reopen at the beginning of April, but the pandemic had other ideas. Our temporary closure quickly became the layoff of over 80 percent of our employees, including me.

Twenty-two years of service and suddenly it was over. Colleagues who have worked at the store longer than I have, employees who've been there less than a year, and everyone in between were suddenly scrambling to understand what was happening. Income zapped. Insurance coming to an end. Medications in limbo. Rents mercilessly approaching. On Facebook, a private page for Powell's union employees was immediately created, where hundreds of bargaining unit members converged to inform and comfort each other. Our union leaders heroically guided people with their unemployment questions and insurance concerns. Many of my coworker friends were angry, heartbroken, and confused by how it all went down. Reading through their posts was gut-wrenching. So many people I saw almost every day, people I loved working with and shared my life with, were now in their own little lifeboats, everyone staying at least six feet away from each other in a crowded sea.

To say that we all feel helpless is an understatement. Not knowing how long this will last, life now becomes a dark limbo. I want to get back to helping customers, recommending books, seeing my friends in the poetry section, and hosting readings for touring authors. I want to put out the rows of chairs and watch them fill. I want to plug in the microphone and tell people to silence their cell phones. I want to go to the Thai restaurant or the food carts for my lunch break and watch basketball highlights at the sports bar after my shift. All those times I told customers where the bathroom was now seem like hallmarks of bygone, halcyon days.

In January, I took eighteen days off to finish a book, and that was the most time I'd had off of work since 1997. During that time, I did wrap up the novel I was writing (my first in eight years) and I also adopted a kitten. Now, those two things—the novel and my kitten, Susan—are three months older, and having eighteen days away from work seems like nothing.

Personal gripes (we'll call them "COVID complaints"), like the stinging thought that agents and editors may hit pause on looking at fiction right now, make me feel self-centered and petty, but I am afraid of what this long quarantine means to the publishing world. I remember how so many great books were ignored in the aftermath of 9/11. In times like these, trying to produce any kind of art feels a bit frivolous. But when we're stuck in our homes and told only to go out when absolutely needed, making art is probably the best way to combat anxiety and atrophy. As Lidia Yuknavitch says, we should all strive to "make art in the face of fuck." I've also used this time to read more, trying to lose myself in my giant to-read piles. And to make some new collages. To watch *The Sopranos* for the first time. To cook and bake more. To listen to new music. And also—okay, mostly!—to spend LOTS of quality time with Susan, who keeps me entertained as only a wild, uncontrollable kitten can.

I'm going to say this as an optimist, and also a realist: we'll get through this and be smarter, stronger, and more grateful because of it. Grateful for books, writing, and art-making, but most of all—for the freedom to gather and share these creations, together.

KEVIN SAMPSELL's writing has appeared in *Paper Darts, Longreads, Salon, Southwest Review,* and elsewhere. He lives in Portland, Oregon, and runs the small press Future Tense Books. He hopes to regain his job as a bookseller and events coordinator for Powell's Books when the quarantine is over.

SAME

By Jamie Ford

As a boy, I was strictly latch-key,
Home alone, the original, not the movie.
One day I found my father's gun, a toy
Fortunately, I never pulled the trigger,
Because blood is a poor stain remover.

As a teen, I was left alone for days on end,
By a working mom whose sweat was 80-proof.
She gave me paperbacks, but I hated her mysteries.
I read comics instead, trading my abandonment
For Spider-Man's issues.

As a man, (what does that even mean?)
I lock myself upstairs, in my office confessional,
Tossing Hail Marys to my imaginary friends,
They whisper their secrets, their fears,
In my ears, that burn at both ends.

As a writer, I wear an old bathrobe, all day,
Like the heroin dealer from *Pulp Fiction*,
Earning my black-belt in daydreaming.
I stare out the window, while a muse
Growls, "Sweep the leg."

I'm lucky though. I get paid twice a year
To stay inside and break my own heart.
I sprinkle glitter on the jagged pieces
And hand them out to strangers,
Seeking their approval.

Homecoming is forever now, for all of us,
Together. Stuck inside, every day's a snow day.
But I'm not lonely, not even a bit.
'Cause we're a pack of introverts,
And every night we howl like wolves.

JAMIE FORD's debut novel, *Hotel on the Corner of Bitter and Sweet*, spent two years on the *New York Times* bestseller list and went on to win the Asian/Pacific American Award for Literature. His work has been translated into thirty-five languages.

FINAL ACT

By Gina Frangello

We didn't even know how to use Zoom an hour ago, but here we were, sending out Zoom invitations to our pop-up wedding. It was supposed to happen in June in California but would instead take place on March 24, 2020, in our Chicago living room, with less than twenty-four hours' notice. Rob and I hadn't even written vows yet. The wedding dress I'd bought for summer needed to be professionally taken up and tailored, so was useless now. The only people who would be in attendance for the ceremony were my three kids from my first marriage, all home with us during the COVID-19 quarantine, and our makeshift officiator: the drummer in Rob's band.

Truth is sometimes described as being surprising at first, but inevitable upon reflection. And the truth is that absolutely nothing—in the eight years of our relationship—had ever gone as planned.

Rob and I met more than twenty years ago when he submitted a short story over the transom to the nonprofit literary magazine I then edited. Over the years, we crossed paths randomly: he was the runner-up in a contest when we launched a book press; we published another story of his in the magazine; finally, we accepted a novel of his for publication, which was released in 2013.

By then we were a year deep in a passionate and clandestine extramarital affair.

———

We had both been married forever—two decades apiece, give or take a few years. Although our marital relationships were radically different, neither of us had ever cheated on our spouses prior to our affair. We spent some three years "ending it" with one another but repeatedly falling back together before finally, reconciled at last to our inability to cleave, we each confessed to our spouses. Though we of course expected a devastating fallout, we had little idea how wide-ranging and brutal the aftermath would truly be.

Rob lived in LA. His literary, music, and recovery communities were all in Southern California, as well as an almost constant sunshine that helped the depression that was a frequent by-product of his ultradian bipolar disorder. I lived in Chicago with my three kids and the two elderly parents I'd been caretaking for nearly a decade. Following the revelation of our affair, my two eldest children understandably wanted nothing to do with Rob. "Do what you want," they told me, "but don't bring him around here." Nine months after I told my ex-husband about the affair—even when he began dating, found a serious relationship, and got engaged—Rob had still never spent a night with me in my family home. We were, plain and simple, homewreckers, and it did not occur to us to challenge my daughters' wishes that he stay away. Rob spent his scant income flying to Chicago for short intervals when we could stay at the "nesting pad" my ex and I time-shared the first nine months of our separation. I rarely wanted to be away from my kids for longer than a few days at a stretch, so Rob would fly to Chicago and then back to his ex's apartment in Southern California with preposterously short turnovers while I worked overtime to normalize my children's lives amid an increasingly contentious divorce. Even when my father—who lived downstairs from us—died, I didn't bring Rob to the memorial service but kept him tucked away at "the pad" out of shame. I was living my life in atonement mode.

Then I got breast cancer. I was diagnosed seven months after my marital separation and two months after my father's death. About six weeks after that, Rob spent the night with me in my family home for the first time and *stayed*—for a month and a half—while I underwent a bilateral radical mastectomy. It was then that my kids were able to see him caring for me—stripping my mastectomy drains and going with me to doctor appointments and doing all the household chores—and slowly began the process of forgiving, accepting, and beginning to bond. My surgery was successful; my margins were clean, and Rob's and my intense attraction and connection had more than survived my body's alteration. When he left Chicago in late February 2016, it was with a plan to move back full-time the following month.

Then, before we could even share our fledgling plans with my children and our friends, his ex also received a diagnosis: breast cancer. The blow was horrifically timed—my MammaPrint and Oncotype DX scores had just come back, unexpectedly, as having a much higher risk for cancer recurrence than my oncologists had anticipated, and suddenly my doctors in Chicago (and a second opinion at Cedars-Sinai) recommended chemotherapy. Rob's ex did not have the support system that I had, so he began a crazy-making period (for us all) of commuting from LA to Chicago, living half-time in each place, taking care of a sick woman and spending his days at medical facilities. Though Rob had been compliant in his treatment for bipolar for many years, in this period his depression escalated into the "red zone," in the words of his LA psychiatrist.

Eventually, his ex and I were each given a good prognosis, and the After we had expected to enter way back in early 2015, when we had first told our spouses about the affair, could begin.

44

At the very end of 2017, Rob moved to Chicago. Soon afterward, I had a full hip replacement (a complication from my chemo), my daughters went off to college—in California, which had by then become our second city—and my beloved mother died. Through all of these hardships, Rob was by my side, holding me up, helping me find laughter, and still making my body surge in ways that defied menopause and the alleged invisibility of the middle-aged American woman.

Rob and I met when we were both youngish, both healthy—when life was as easy as it was ever going to be. Now here we were, in the middle of a global pandemic, my daughters back from California to shelter in place with us, our youngest child home from a shuttered elementary school. Then Rob's divorce papers suddenly arrived in the mail. Amid the terror that our government would not protect us and our medical system would collapse under the weight of COVID-19, all we wanted was to be married—to face this crucible together as husband and wife.

"Are you sure you don't want to get married in California later on?" I asked more than once. "You can add me and the kids to your insurance as a domestic partner now that you're divorced. We don't need to get married right away." There were practical reasons to marry—the HMO that both my youngest child and I were on had been a cause of concern since the virus began casting its shadow; we could only be seen at one medical facility, and already they were overwhelmed. Still, Rob had changed his entire life to be with me, and California remained a magical place to him, where he yearned to celebrate our wedding with his longtime community at a beach ceremony followed by an offbeat reception at his favorite dive bar.

"I don't care about any of that," he reassured me, smiling at me

45

while the world collapsed around us. "I'm marrying *you*. I'm the luckiest man in the world."

"At least do it on Zoom!" a close California friend admonished us, to which we mutually groaned, "We don't understand Zoom." And so he walked us through it, then and there, the night before the wedding. Of the eighty-two Zoom invites we hastily sent, some seventy friends and family "attended" the following evening at 5:30 p.m., weak, half-gray Chicago daylight still lighting our living room. I chose a dress I'd worn on our dream trip to Paris, along with my daughter's Doc Martens combat boots; Rob wore a too-big blazer one of his students had once taken off and given him impromptu at a party. Some of our virtual guests donned swanky hats and long white gloves with their pajama bottoms. And there in our shared home, in front of so many people who had witnessed our journey—both the harrowing and the beautiful parts—we promised to have each other's backs, to be each other's final acts, and, as Rob tells me every day, never to take a moment of our incredible life together for granted.

The day after our wedding, Rob, who had sick on and off since early March and had already tested negative for the flu, grew sicker. He soon developed the fever, the dry cough and wheezing, the fatigue, and the head and neck pain associated with COVID-19. I've been ill too, though less severely—I am able to sit here at my computer, writing this, while he has spent his days mainly sleeping. While neither of us is in the highest-risk group, we are also not young and both have underlying medical conditions. We fully hope and expect to outlast this turbulent period in world history—to be standing on the other side among those who remember together—but in our story of the unexpected, taking nothing for granted also entails a full understanding of the transience and impermanence of life.

Part of why we traveled this arduous road, when either one of us had plenty of cause at any moment to reverse course and give up, was precisely for this reason: in our darkest hour, we are now exactly where we want to be.

GINA FRANGELLO is the author of four books of fiction, most recently the novels *A Life in Men* and *Every Kind of Wanting*. Her debut book of nonfiction, *Blow Your House Down*, will be released in 2021.

NIGHT TIDE

By N. L. Shompole

On Saturday, I dredge the bog that settled in my stomach some-time in April. I watch movies in a hazmat suit, breath clouding the plastic screen, consumed by the fog brought on by memory. I play at exorcism, taking turns to excise each memory—like fishing for the drowned deep in the marshes, the movie on screen long forgotten. Each submersion aches and burns in turns, wrecking me, leaving me a wailing, trembling mass on the sofa.

It is delicate work, sinking elbow deep into despair—heart hammer-ing in tandem with the tide. Washing over me in slow, melancholic waves that work me over and under, until I can't tell sea from sky from land anymore.

*

Am I dreaming, or remembering? I cannot tell the difference any-more. What I know is that each memory is a bloated body washed ashore from some distant wreckage.

When I come up for air it is to the blare of the fire-alarm ringtone and rolling credits on the screen. Shoulders aching from the weight of the haunting, and the effort it takes to continually sift through memory in search of a refuge island to rest on. There are no footholds to be found in the gathering dark.

*

This must be what it feels like to be consumed by sorrow.

Me, wrapped up in yellow plastic hotter
than a years' worth of sun.

Me, strangled by the howl nested in my chest.

Me, lost somewhere between you and the future
we imagined for ourselves.

∗

Sometimes I think I like myself better this way. A body wrapped up
in the strange afterglow brought on by sorrow. The dark nestles tight
around me like a blanket. Vice-grip around the bird trying to crawl
out of my throat.

I do not want to be found.

N.L. SHUMPOLE is the author of the bestselling poetry collection
Lace Bone Beast: Poems & Other Fairytales for Wicked Girls (2017).
Her most recent work includes the Eugie Award-nominated short story
"Strangers Tomorrow," which was published in the anthology
[Dis]Connected (2019).

PART TWO: GRIEVE

IN CONVERSATION WITH DAVID SHEFF

"We can treat our pain and create change when we turn our anger into
action, connect with others, and do our best to help those in need . . ."

Reading David Sheff's memoir *Beautiful Boy*, about surviving the decade in which his family faced the addiction of his teenaged son, Nic, I was deeply moved by Sheff's detailed description of the phases of grief he went through over losing the son he thought he knew so well. He went through depression, anger, and finally found the compassion necessary to help both his son and himself—and then others. His research into substance-use disorders led to two more books, and he's also an activist, speaking at community meetings, with healthcare professionals, at colleges, and elsewhere about the impact of addiction. Most recently, he created the Beautiful Boy Fund, a nonprofit devoted to making available quality, evidence-based addiction care and supporting research to further the field of addiction medicine.

Sheff's desire to turn his grief outward toward helping others was partially inspired by five years of conversations with a death-row inmate, Jarvis Jay Masters, a story Sheff documents in his new book, *The Buddhist on Death Row*. Wrongfully convicted of involvement in the murder of a prison guard, Masters spent two decades in solitary confinement in San Quentin. During that period he transformed from a man consumed by rage and violence to one who devotes his life to helping others find meaning and peace. Here's more from Sheff about transforming grief into activism.

Jennifer Haupt: You went through ten years of trying and failing to help your son, Nic, as his addiction to methamphetamine and other drugs nearly killed him. Did you know at the time that you were grieving?

David Sheff: Part of the trauma and suffering of all those years was from the loss of who my son had been. The open, kind, gentle, moral, beautiful boy I had raised was gone. On drugs, he became un-recognizable—breaking into our home and stealing, verbally abusive, literally out of his mind. I felt a combination of terror and this deep, dark sadness that is grief, and I learned that grief can paralyze or mo-tivate. It's not that different from what we are feeling now as a coun-try. So many of us, across political, racial, and socioeconomic lines, are grieving, but the question is how we'll deal with it all. Will it paralyze us or motivate us?

JH: There was a point in your relationship with Nic where you went from a state of paralyzing depression to anger. We're seeing that now, sparked by the brutal murder of George Floyd by Minneapolis police offi-cers. Was that anger useful for you?

DS: I went from being numb to feeling an overwhelming sense of fear and frustration about my inability to solve a problem that was ruining the lives of everyone I loved. Anger came next. I thought, *How can Nic do this to us? To me? To himself?* I lashed out at my son, my ex-wife, even my wife Karen. At my worst, I was unable to be fully present for my younger kids. I was confused. Looking back, I realize I needed to experience the confusion, loss, grief, and anger for me to face Nic's addiction in a useful way. Over time, those debilitating emotions morphed from judgment and anger to compassion. It was compassion, not judgment, anger, and shame, that helped him. We're lucky. Nic survived. He's been in recovery for eleven years.

JH: How do you account for being able to move through your grief instead of staying stuck in it? That can go either way, right?

DS: I frequently hear from parents whose kids are currently addicted or have died of overdose. Some of them are consumed by pain and bitterness; they live in a state of hell. I don't judge them. I understand. I've been right there with them. But then there are people whose grief evolves into a useful kind of anger. Many of those who die of addiction do so because they've been failed by what passes for a mental-health care system in America. They also die because of the stigma of addiction—they keep their problem hidden because of shame—until there are devastating consequences. "Oh, he's just a junkie." An ER nurse told me she hears doctors say it all the time. Many are deprived of addiction medications that could save their lives.

Many parents or other loved ones recognize the broken system and determine to do whatever they can to prevent others from having to endure the suffering they've endured. They're passionately committed to improving the treatment system, educating about addiction, and lobbying legislators for support for those suffering mental illness. The ability to create change, even it comes a small shift at a time, is empowering. No parent will ever stop grieving the loss of a child, but these men and women find new purpose.

JH: We're now seeing that shift of grief, from depression to sheer anger, to compassionate activism happening en masse. Of course, we've seen this before with racial equality. From your perspective as a journalist, is this period in history different?

DS: During the past four years, since 2016, we've become used to having our optimism crushed again and again. It began with Trump's election and has been followed by the horrors perpetrated by his administration. Then came the murder of George Floyd. The movement was motivated by the video of his sickening murder. It's not the first video that showed black men and women murdered by police, but it was the straw that broke the camel's back. It unleashed simmering rage.

I see change coming. I hope I'm not naïve. There will be fierce opposition, but laws are being enacted and the nation is rethinking criminal justice and policing. The Black Lives Matter movement is unstoppable. The near universal outrage will, hopefully, inspire more people to vote, and we'll take the country back from those who are destroying our democracy. I'm optimistic, but I'm also bracing for the crisis that will come if Trump wins. He could lose the popular vote again, but, because of voter suppression and God knows what dirty tricks, still win. If that happens, I don't know how we'll handle the disappointment. Will we keep fighting? How can we keep ourselves from being overtaken by anger and bitterness?

JH: This is a good time to turn the conversation toward Jarvis Masters. How did you decide to write about him?

DS: We had a mutual friend, one of his spiritual teachers, who told me that in spite of being locked up in San Quentin for twenty-five years, twenty of them in solitary confinement, he wasn't bitter or hateful. He'd become a Buddhist and taught Buddhism to other inmates. He'd written a book, *Finding Freedom*, that circulated widely and helped kids on the outside avoid gangs and violence. He also helped inmates and guards by teaching them empathy. I was cynical at first, but I researched his case and became convinced he was on death row for a crime he didn't commit.

I confirmed the stories I'd heard. Jarvis had become a *bodhisattva*, one who works to alleviate suffering in a place drowning in suffering. He had every reason to be bitter and full of rage—he grew up that way. And yet he changed, and his bitterness and anger evolved into compassion. I decided to write about him, partly to explore questions many of us want to ask: Can people change? And, if we can, how do we do that?

JH: What did you learn from Jarvis and the principles of Buddhism?

DS: I'm not a Buddhist—I'm not religious at all—but I learned a lot about the ways Buddhist practices and teachings can help anyone, believers and nonbelievers alike. I learned how embracing the universality of suffering leads, paradoxically, to less suffering. I learned that you have to face, not run from, whatever you struggle with. As one of Jarvis's teachers said, "The only way out is through." Another of Jarvis's teachers—his first, a lama from Tibet—said, "We're all in prison, and we all have the key." The key is facing ourselves. It's the dissolution of ego, which separates us from rather than connects us with humanity and causes endless suffering. It's opening up to others by recognizing their suffering and feeling it. And it's helping others. Jarvis entered San Quentin at age nineteen for armed robbery, not trusting anyone, filled with rage. That rage helped him survive an abusive and violent childhood and the violence of the juvenile justice system and then prison. But he changed in prison. One day he was on the yard, watching shirtless men lifting weights. He noticed that all the men had scars on their backs and legs from being whipped and beaten as children. They were like his own scars. He said, "It's as if we all had the same parents." It was the first time he recognized others' suffering and connected it with his own. He came to the heart of Buddhism.

JH: How has activism changed grief for you?

DS: Over the years since I first wrote about Nic's addiction, I've connected with more and more parents going through their own kids' drug problems, mental illnesses, depression, and other challenges. I also met many parents whose beautiful boys and girls died, often of overdose or suicide. At first, meeting these people, experiencing their grief, overwhelmed me. I became depleted and depressed. At one point, however, Jarvis talked about something that changed me. I recognized that in order to protect myself from others' pain, I'd put up a wall between these people and me. I tried to protect myself from absorbing their pain and drowning in it. But that wall isolated me from them and from myself.

I began to look at them differently—to *see* them. What I saw was their humanity. In their sadness and pain, I saw their beauty. I saw how we're all connected. We're all in the same boat. When we see that, we're compelled to do what we can to help one another. That's where activism comes from. We do what we can to alleviate suffering. It's happening now in America. We can get depressed about the pandemic and systemic racism, but like the parents whose kids die of addiction who become activists, our grief can lead to action. We stand up against injustice. Jarvis taught me about engaged Buddhism, and I think this is what it's all about: We can treat our pain and create change when we turn our grief and anger into action.

DAVID SHEFF is the author of the bestsellers *Beautiful Boy* and *Clean.* His most recent book is *The Buddhist on Death Row.*

I KIND OF WANT TO LOVE THE WORLD, BUT I HAVE NO IDEA HOW TO HOLD IT

By Kelli Russell Agodon and Melissa Studdard

I'm dazed already, I'm over-chocolated
and writing poems to a universe that

keeps wrapping its constellations around
my waist, wrapping its tragedies

around the necks of entire planets. I've
seen hungers so desperate they can

never be filled. Stray children. Stray dogs.
My stray self. I tried to hold it all—

stuffed more and more in until my container
broke. Skin and glass everywhere.

Little shards of me on the floor, mixed
with everyone and everything else

that is broken. Mixed too with the tragic,
beautiful worlds that spilled out like

secret eggs from which, I was certain, some
lovely, winged creature would emerge.

Kelli Russell Agodon is a poet, writer, editor, book designer, and cofounder of Two Sylvias Press. Her work has appeared in *The Atlantic; The Nation;* and *O, The Oprah Magazine.* Her fourth collection of poems, *Dialogues with Rising Tides,* will be published in 2021.

Melissa Studdard is the author of five books, including the poetry collection *I Ate the Cosmos for Breakfast* and the young adult novel *Six Weeks to Yehidah.* Her work has appeared in the *New York Times, POETRY, Kenyon Review, Psychology Today, The Guardian, New Ohio Review, Harvard Review, New England Review* and *Poets & Writers.*

BREATHING LILACS

By Laura Stanfill

Kitchen Chair

You don't know a place until you've seen it in different seasons, and behold: spring! Everything blooms in surprising waves of color at my parents' place. Their new house is a six-minute drive from ours, but my mom and dad are still three thousand miles away, sheltering in the place they plan to leave. Same quarantine, different furniture. I hunt for dishes in their kitchen, carry a few boxes up their stairs, take long steamy baths in their tub, check for ants in their laundry room, pull their weeds. Daffodils unfurl, followed by tulips, then extravagant blooms of pink dogwood, orange azalea, and a high-crowned shrub of lilacs. New leaves appear on the patio trellis vine. Grapes? In the rain, I drag a kitchen chair outside, stand on my tiptoes, and snip a fragrant purple clump to carry indoors.

Shawl

Priya gave me a red and gray shawl for my birthday in early March. She had it monogrammed with the letter *L* for *Laura*. I told her I couldn't imagine a more perfect stay-at-home present. It's even machine washable. When I sent her a photo of me wearing the shawl while reading to my daughters, Priya said, *Did they forget the monogram?* I texted a photo of the *L* in gold, then wrapped myself back up in it, waited for her response.

Seeds

My friend Amy offers extras to anyone who wants to pick them up. Green beans and golden beans. Chard. Butter lettuce. Summer squash. A reason to venture outside our neighborhood: also a gift. Amy leaves the seeds, a bucket of potting soil, and a stack of egg cartons on her step. A contactless arrangement. She tops the gift with a platter of warm cookies. At home, my daughters and I take the packets out and pour new life into our palms, sort each into its own cardboard nest.

Phone

When the virus depleted Priya's oxygen levels, nobody could ride with her in the ambulance because of the risk of contagion. Melissa and Justin, her other two best friends, live in New Jersey, same as Priya. They could have visited her bedside in ordinary times. Instead, the three of us relied on Priya's sisters for news, trading texts with each other, asking, *Anything today?*

Cape

Cast on. Knit two rows. Loop yarnovers for a ribbon row. Am I too old for a red cape with a white satin ribbon? It doesn't matter. The wool scratches my dry, over-washed hands. I knit and increase, purling on the back. I cannot get on a plane, so this is how I wait for news of Priya. With my fingers. They swell and grow sore, but I don't stop. Something has to carry me forward into the next ten minutes, the next hour. It might as well be a woolen red cape.

Sourdough Starter

We named ours Robin, after Robin Sloan, author of a novel about a magical starter. I bake crackers, hot pretzels, and bread with Robin, whose pronouns, my daughters insist, are she/her. I feed Robin and whisper words of encouragement, urging her to grow, so she can feed us. I think of Priya's chai. She makes the best chai. It would go well with the tang of sourdough. I wish I could bring her fresh-baked crackers.

Satin

The day Priya gets intubated and put on a ventilator, my girls and I stuff messages of kindness into skinny satin bags with lace ruffs. A friend sewed these bags for my wedding, nearly twenty years ago now. I find the stash of remainders in a cupboard in the laundry room. They are strange colors—forest green, bathroom pink, a theatrical purple. *There is hope in the world,* my eight-year-old writes on a paper rectangle. We add pompoms, red felt hearts, paste jewels, stickers. The girls and I tie eleven bags on the back fence, along a busy street. *Need hope? Take one. Stay safe,* my twelve-year-old writes with a waterproof black marker. She attaches the paper sign to the fence with pipe cleaners. It doesn't matter if people take bags or not. What matters: the word *hope.*

Magazine

Any page will do for today's homeschool art lessons. I grab *Popular Mechanics* because my girls don't want it. I rip out a page, circle a few elements to keep, then slather the rest with acrylic paint. Once it dries, I draw Priya with straight bangs and long hair, the way I remember her from fifth grade. I cut out a beach umbrella in case she needs some shade. I put a blue paper cloud over her face, because I can't draw faces, but that's too sad, so I move it down and add more clouds, so the first one doesn't get lonely. The migrating cloud leaves a streak of pink glitter paint on her face, and it's nice like that, so I leave it.

Something White

The news comes from her sister like all the other updates these past two weeks: by text. A friend reports it's appropriate to wear white to Priya's funeral, so Justin, Melissa, and I hunt in our closets. I find a gauzy scarf with bronze embroidered flowers, pair it with a white and gray paisley dress with hints of gold. I go to my parents' house to attend the funeral. Our cameras are off; we are all on mute. The priest sings prayers. The family sprinkles Priya's white casket with petals and spices. The funeral home workers wheel her away. One isn't wearing a mask. The family follows the body, singing prayers and wailing. We keep watch over the empty room until someone thinks to turn us off.

Bed

My twelve-year-old daughter stops getting out of bed. She won't even get up to try on the red cape, which on me, strains a little at the buttonholes. She writes to her teacher: "I feel so alone because I have no one my age to hang out with and my mom is in deep grief cause of her friend dying and my sister not being herself cause the grief rubbed off on me and my sister so I have been hiding from everyone because I don't no how to deal with my mom when she is griefing." I ask her to send me this sentence, because it goes on and on, just like how it feels to miss someone you've known for thirty years.

Charm

I am walking a virtual Camino de Santiago with two thousand pilgrims, led by my travel-writer friend Gigi. It's standard, she tells our group, to bring a memento to leave behind when you have lost a loved one. Wrapped in the red and gray shawl Priya gave me, I check on the satin bags in the backyard—six left—and then loop a tiny purple Hello Kitty charm around the fence by the pear tree. I bought the charm for Priya at a local comic-book shop and never got around to mailing it to her. Hello Kitty is hidden, away from the *take one* sign, but if someone wants it, that's okay.

Cupcakes

My neighbor and I haven't spoken since the pandemic started. We used to take daily walks but now, when I wave from across the street, Chrysia turns her head and doesn't wave back. I think she's hurting. Or maybe she senses I am. I make her a birthday card out of paper scraps and glue, take a photo with my phone, and text it over with a question. Does she approve of no-contact food delivery, and if so, would she want me to order cupcakes for her? "Best birthday present of the day," she responds. I fill the virtual bakery cart with rainbow cupcakes and macarons decorated like pugs, then send her a text with the estimated delivery time. Not that she's going anywhere.

Dried Apricots

Priya's father dies from the virus eight days after she does. The news: another text. Two more names for the list of doctors who have lost their lives to the pandemic. It's a rainy day on the virtual Camino. I admit to carrying this fresh, secondary grief. People I don't know, other pilgrims, are willing to walk this stretch with me. One suggests she can help with the weight by carrying my pack for a while. I am offered sips of hot mint tea, dried apricots. I put one foot in front of the other in the tall wet grass behind my parents' house. We need to bring our mower over. The grass soaks my sneakers. I breathe lilacs.

LAURA STANFILL is the publisher of Forest Avenue Press. She believes in indie bookstores and wishes on them like stars.

RIVER OF GRIEF

By Grace Talusan

The one constant for me during this pandemic is grief. Grief is an underground river running beneath every waking moment and every activity I do—or no longer do—in order to distract myself. I grieve for the regular things I've lost, from sitting in crowded cafés to cooking with my nephew to sharing an XL bowl of pho with my parents at the Vietnamese restaurant halfway between our homes, and the once-in-a-lifetime things, my first book's paperback tour. Something will remind me of someone I've known or loved who has died and I plunge into this cold river. I'm not so overwhelmed that my day is ruined, but the feeling is strong enough that I stop whatever I'm doing and sit with the memory of my dead—who they were to me, all they gave to me, and who I was in their presence.

Day after day, the memory of a beloved floats past me, reminders that they are dead. Reminders that someday I will die, too.

———

I went to the Philippines the summer after my first year of graduate school because my grandmother was dying. It was my third time in the country of my birth since leaving for America at age two. Sometimes I wonder if the act of migration was the river's original source. What did that rupture from my first language, my loved ones, and my home country do to me? The narrative of migration is often expressed as a one-way move toward a better life, but what and who did I lose by leaving my so-called "bad" life in the Philippines?

Does the multiverse contain the Filipino version of me?

We were not able to visit for twenty years because we needed to fix our immigration status. I did not know much about the Philippines, so when my grandmother would stay with us for months at a time, she brought our country to us. I tasted the Philippines through snacks, dried watermelon seeds and crunchy fried corn kernels, and imagined this place through stories from my grandmother. She would braid my hair every night and tie it with white rags torn from an old T-shirt. When I sat between her legs as she parted my hair into sections and tied it into black ropes, I felt normal for once, like one of the American girls in the books I read.

When the end was near, my grandmother was moved to a former convent and set up in a hospital bed in the lobby outside of the chapel door so that a stream of visitors—nine children and their spouses, dozens of grandchildren, other relations, friends, and colleagues from all over the world—could visit with her and then walk steps away to the chapel to keep their promise to pray for her soul's repose.

Interacting with her during this time, I often felt as if I were participating in one of her dreams. She raised her arms and waved them, eyes closed as she conducted an orchestra the way she had as a young woman. She bicycled her legs and asked me to follow her to the attic to retrieve her winter clothes from the suitcase she stored in my parents' New England home. She chewed imaginary meals, opening and closing her mouth. Without her dentures in, I was startled to see her remaining teeth, so tiny and mustard-colored, ground into stubs.

When she was awake, she would acknowledge the people sitting beside me: her husband, her father, her son Eddie, and her sisters. All of them were long deceased. I was told that when we're close to death, our ancestors appear to accompany us on the journey to the afterlife.

A few years later, my aunt, the whites of her eyes bright yellow from her failing liver, would see the grandchild who'd been a baby when he died, and hear a choir of angels from her deathbed. A day or so before she stopped speaking, my aunt woke up to say that her brother, who was sleeping in another bedroom down the hallway, was shivering from the air conditioning, and could someone give him a blanket? The explanation was that my aunt's soul was already leaving her body and roaming to places in the house that her body could not walk to.

I was always taught that I have a soul which will live on after my body dies. After death, the soul wanders the earth until the fortieth day, an auspicious number for Christians, their judgment day. At the celebration for Lolo Bien, a deceased elder of the family, my two-year-old nephew Gavin suddenly pointed to the chair at the head of the table and announced, "Lolo there." Through hand gestures and the few words he could speak, Gavin communicated that Lolo Bien, clothed in white, was sitting in the chair, appearing and disappearing. There was Lolo, waving hello to Gavin. And then he'd hide and come back again, smiling and making the child laugh. When Lolo Bien's family heard this story, they made the sign of the cross. The story left them both delighted and grief-stricken. Even though Gavin was too young to know our beliefs about the afterlife, he confirmed them. Their father was still here. He had shown himself.

My mother told me stories about loved ones who died unexpectedly and sent a text message or left a voicemail after their official time of death. Two recently deceased relatives showed up in reminder messages on her social media and email. (*Do you want to reply to your message to Ronnie? Do you want to share your memory with Ramon?*) She interpreted these technological glitches as messages from loved ones, reaching out from the beyond to remind her she was loved.

All of these visitations by deceased family members are comforting proof that death is not the end, that there are stories about our loved ones existing outside of the body, beyond explanation.

————

When I first heard these kinds of stories as a girl, I didn't have a choice: I believed my mother. Other relatives and Filipino immigrants told their own ghostly tales about interaction with our dead, and our white Christian friends believed in Heaven too.

Growing up in America and attending secular schools where talk of God and the supernatural was disdained—the territory of backward ignorant fools—I wanted to ally myself with the educated and powerful. I know what the scientific method is and how to support an argument with evidence. How to think critically. And yet I want to believe that our connection to our loved ones extends beyond their deaths. That sometimes in their new lives, they think of us and flicker the lights or play music or waft a scent—their perfume or favorite flower—or appear as a bird every morning on our porch. In some way, they give us a sign, especially when we are in despair. They remind us that we are loved. I choose to believe this story. It makes me feel better, not so alone, and how can that be wrong?

I think my dead are appearing to me now, during the quarantine, because finally I have the time to grieve them. They must be so mad at me; how I pretended to move on so quickly from the gravity and finality of their deaths. I did not make room in my life to properly grieve. I never felt I could stop working long enough to do so. When I would inform students and coworkers that I needed time off for loved ones' funerals, I apologized, full of shame for not being available to work.

How wrong I was to model this inflexibility.

But now, because everyone is staying at home, I am not jumping out of bed after a poor night's sleep and driving around town and teaching and emailing, so many emails, and having in-person meetings, appointments, and coffee dates; basically, proving that I am a worthy person in American society because I am productive for every waking moment. What event in your life could be bigger and more profound than dying? If I've learned anything during these months at home, it is that I am not a machine. I am human and I will attend to this humanness.

A few weeks into the pandemic, we lost a lifelong friend to COVID-19. She was like an aunt to me. Last year, even though she was still recovering from knee surgery, she insisted on cooking Filipino party food for two hundred guests at my book launch party. She worked in produce in a grocery store and often gave us bags of fruit, somehow finding the sweetest cherries in the store. The virus took her so quickly—she was at home coughing and then in the ICU and then her kidneys were failing and then she was gone.

Her daughter was given an urn. This was her mother now. We could not gather around her body and pray. We could not hug the family she left behind. There are reasons humans have death rituals and because we could not have them, it's hard to believe she's really gone. All we have of her now are stories, which find a way into our conversations, even if this remembering is only one sentence long: "No one could find sweet cherries like her."

How does one cope when all the people who loved you best, one by one, disappear forever? Maybe you tell yourself a story.

GRACE TALUSAN is the author of the memoir *The Body Papers*, winner of the Restless Books Prize for New Immigrant Writing and a *New York Times* Editors' Choice selection. She is the Fannie Hurst Writer-in-Residence at Brandeis University.

BILLOW OF THISTLES

By Ruben Quesada

I have only ever left this planet once in a billow of thistles
after snorting meth amphetamine
in an abandoned record store

in Hollywood, birds settling into the window sills.

A man whom I was engaged to
left me to take communion
with a Jesuit order in Ireland.
From Christ's dress a thread spun itself into the body of Adam

at his feet. From out of his palm the translucent figure of Eve.

I never heard from him again.

The salmon-colored sky eagerly held the night back long enough for
them to recognize their flaws.

RUBEN QUESADA is the author of *Revelations* (Sibling Rivalry Press, 2018). He serves as a blogger at the *Kenyon Review* and as poetry editor at *AGNI*.

SKIN

By Paulette Perhach

From that close up, he looked like my entire world. Around his eyes, the tiny folds that led to lashes. The cove behind his earlobe, where my lips loved to land. His sweet inner arm, where in our bed I made my home.

This was the language we spoke. I'd give him the look, he'd pat the skin above his heart, and I'd relax into the person I've always been, inhaling all that it means to be human. I needed it, but he never made me feel needy.

Skin, remember? Everywhere, warmth, from my cheek on his neck to the scarf of his arms around my back, the whole of him against the whole of me, hip bone to my belly button, foot vined around his ankle. A touch-drunk junkie for this, I forgot everything else I had to do.

Once, I walked into our bedroom to see him lying on his side, eyelids still closed as he reached his palm out and held his hand over the air of my bed space, then lowered it, searching for me so, so, softly, as if I were a thing he might crush.

My mother had this dream about my father. Twenty years after his death, on a night we happened to be visiting, she reached out for him, and the sheets collapsed in her touch.

How lucky to stand there, alive to see it. I'd always wanted a love like theirs.

In the mornings, I started my day by writing three things I was thankful for. Almost every day, he was the most obvious choice. When he called my own mother *Mom*, some part of me, on vigil my entire life, finally closed its eyes and rested.

But then he left.

To skin is a thing you can do. To peel, to leave nerves exposed.

He said I'm selfish. I fear this about myself. I try to fight that part of me, submerge it under the person I want to be. But, even to keep him, I failed.

Just as suddenly, skin is where the virus is, fading into my life as he fades out. Skin is what carries it from them to me, from me to them. Skin is what lets it in.

I tried to get him to quarantine with me, tried to sneak back into my world, but he only texted back, We shouldn't be doing this. I asked him if he was sure, about everything, and he said yes. He said sorry.

I arrived at my friend's house one last time before lockdown. "I'm not doing hugs," he said, hands up at my outstretched arms.

The next day, in a temporary rented room, I sat on someone else's twin bed and unpacked my fraction of our home, with so many reasons to touch my face.

Touch, the first language my mother taught me as an infant, gone mute. Her face now a flat rectangle of worry. Why don't I come home for a bit, she asked. It would cost so little to fly there, if there weren't the chance it might cost so much.

Can you hear me? You're frozen.

I was saying what it's like, trying to live without the heat of him in the morning, without that first hug, without a place to rest my head watching TV. Without handholding, his thumb whispering arcs on my skin, without walking up behind him as he cooked dinner, my chin on his shoulder, wishing people lived forever.

And now, without even the arms of friends who might comfort

me, without the shoulder they might allow me when I try to remember what I used to do with my hands before him, and my voice catches, my eyes flood.

I can hear you but I can't see you. Can you hear me?

Without my friend's dog on my lap. Without my friend's kiddo when she calls my name, runs to me and jumps into my arms, where I sneak the joy of her cheek with a squeeze before I let her down to play. Without even the tip of a friend's fingers clinging to mine as we spin on the dance floor, still dumped and too drunk but at least not alone.

Just me in the grocery store, shopping for one, as lonely and rejected as the last bag of gluten-free buckwheat flour on an empty shelf.

No, I can hear you.

Stupid, it was so stupid. In a slap to my own face, I returned, defeated, to the app where he first read that I'm a cuddler. Deleted the words that had become our inside jokes. Wrote new ones. Deleted the first photos he ever saw of me, the last I thought I'd ever have to post there. Replaced them.

He saw. Took that to mean it didn't matter at all, though it mattered so much that the weakest parts of me slithered toward any cheap, pixelated replacement to ease the rawness of my hands, gasping at the air.

And that, more certainly than ever, was that.

Hello? Did I lose you?

Now, with just the grit of regret between my teeth, I feel banished, feel only the numb glass of my phone in the morning, feel shock detonate through my chest like my skin might visibly cave. Feel unentitled to grief when so many are dying alone. Feel like he's the only one I want to hold me through all this. Of everything I can't touch, he's the furthest away.

Skin. It's the line drawn around us. What's pressed between us. What holds us in. How will I go on without it?

Arms crossed around myself, head down as if bracing against a cold for which I did not plan, there's nothing to do but find out.

PAULETTE PERHACH is a freelance writer and writing coach who has been published in the *New York Times*, *Elle*, *Marie Claire*, *Yoga Journal*, and *Hobart*. Her book *Welcome to the Writer's Life* was selected as one of *Poets & Writers'* Best Books for Writers.

TOUCH

By Michelle Goodman

I. LIFE

My once-healthy ox of a husband slumped over in the wheelchair, snoring gently. It was 2016. Greg was forty-seven, dying of cancer, and for the past two days more asleep than awake.

I'd put off washing his hair all weekend. The hours had been crowded with visits from loved ones who'd traveled many miles to hold his hand, rub his back, tell him how much he meant to them. The morning winter sky filled with Seattle's trademark gray mist. The last thing in the world I wanted to do was wash my husband's sweat-drenched head. I'd spent the past hour helping Greg to and from the bathroom, getting his pills and morphine into him, putting a fresh pair of pajamas on him, changing the sheets on his rented hospital bed, doing the laundry. I would have killed for ninety consecutive minutes of sleep. And when was the last time I had eaten or showered or smelled anything other than the sickly sweet scent of decay filling that TV-room-turned-death-portal?

The day's parade of visitors was set to start in half an hour, though, and I was determined to stay on task. I grabbed a magic, self-washing shower cap the hospice nurse had brought us the week before and willed myself to make sense of the instructions: *Place the cap on the patient's head, massage for two to three minutes, and voilà! Clean hair, no rinsing or toweling off needed.*

The baby-blue plastic packaging listed only two ingredients: aloe vera and rubbing alcohol. I wondered if self-washing shower caps worked as magically as the packaging claimed. Perhaps the hospice center didn't give a shit if the dying were left with shampoo residue in their hair. They were *dying*.

I made sure Greg's wheelchair brakes were locked and then stood behind him. The sound of me tearing open the wrapper awakened him, the way our dog would stir from her bed when I opened food packaging in the kitchen. As I fit the shower cap onto Greg's scalp, he lifted his head off his chest, struggling to hold it up.

I couldn't keep Greg alive. But I could try to keep him clean and comfortable. Although I wasn't convinced his hair was cleaner after I removed the cap, it had the illusion of cleanliness, or at least fresh-ness—the somewhat antiseptic scent of the gooey aloe-and-alcohol combination preferable to the tangy, bitter smell of perspiration.

"Are you gonna cut my hair now?" Greg asked, confusing me with the friend scheduled to give him a trim later that week.

I bit the inside of my mouth, willed myself not to cry. "No, baby, I just washed your hair," I said, tracing one of the damp, overgrown curls creeping down the base of his neck with my index finger.

My husband's chin fell onto his chest. He'd already fallen back asleep.

II. DEATH

The next morning Greg was gone. No breath, no heartbeat, the pulse oximeter I'd purchased at the drugstore weeks earlier showing no signs of life. Unsure what to do, I called 911. Paramedics and po-lice soon crowded our TV room and confirmed what I didn't want to be true. Someone turned off the humming oxygen concentrator in the hall and removed the nasal cannula from Greg's face.

"Please don't take him away," I pleaded. "The hospice told me I could keep him home for twenty-four more hours."

No one objected.

After the entourage left, I called the hospice. A nurse offered to come help wash Greg's body. Together we slipped him out of his clammy pajamas and, with towels and a plastic basin, gently bathed and dried him. We then maneuvered him into a fresh pair of lounge pants and his favorite football jersey, black and purple nylon emblazoned with his name in white letters on the back. Greg was still warm. His skin was soft and supple.

My sister came over midmorning, just as the nurse was leaving. She made camp upstairs, fielding calls and texts, while I stayed in the TV room with my husband. I grabbed the CD remote and hit play. The carousel was filled with Beatles and Dylan discs Greg had chosen days earlier, his favorites. I curled up alongside him, sobbing, squeezing his arms, petting his hair, kissing his lips and cheeks and eyelids, telling him how sorry I was that he had to go.

I took pictures of Greg's serene, handsome face. I listened to songs like "Simple Twist of Fate" and "You're a Big Girl Now" as though hearing them for the first time. This went on well into the afternoon, save for the couple of times my sister came downstairs to bring me food or relay messages from relatives.

The back of Greg's neck grew a mottled purple as the blood inside his body began to pool. His skin was cooling, his limbs stiffening. I wondered aloud if I should call the funeral home to come get him.

"Take your time," my sister said, touching my arm. "There's no rush."

"After this CD," I told her. "I'll be ready then."

I listened to *Abbey Road* one final time with my husband, wondering if he'd purposefully placed it last in the carousel so I'd hear The Beatles singing about the love you take being equal to the love you make while I kissed him goodbye.

III. AFTERLIFE

I periodically visit the cemetery where Greg is buried, my rituals a lot like those from our last day together: I talk to him and cry. I play wistful songs on my phone. I bring him shells and rocks from the beach. I lay in the soft grass with my cheek pressed against his cool headstone. Only now I do all this wearing a mask.

Sometimes I look across the cemetery grounds to the chapel, the site of Greg's memorial more than three years ago. A hundred people stuffed into that overheated sanctuary to share juicy bear hugs, little-known stories about Greg, and deep belly laughs. We sat shoulder to shoulder in the pews, passing programs and tissues and cups of water. My brother-in-law, who officiated, clasped hands with each person who stepped to the podium to speak. When the slideshow of photos grew too much for me to bear, my mother locked elbows with me and my sister interlaced her fingers with mine, anchoring my body to the pew.

After the service, the crowd spilled into the reception area. The sea of neighbors, friends, family, and colleagues from various eras of our life was dizzying. We squeezed hands and passed around old photo albums and ate from communal platters of finger food. I wasn't sure when, if ever, I'd see them again in one setting, so I pressed my cheeks to as many of them as I could. I savored each embrace, our tears and breath and words of comfort comingling like morning mist and fog before evaporating in the sunlight.

MICHELLE GOODMAN is author of *The Anti 9-to-5 Guide* and *My So-Called Freelance Life*. Her essays have appeared in the *Washington Post, Seattle Times, Salon, Narratively,* and several anthologies.

THE LAST T-SHIRT

By Julie Gardner

I still have the last t-shirt he ever wore
the one he took off before he went to bed
the black one he took off on that Friday night
that July Friday night when the full moon was eclipsed
I see it puddled on the stained tan carpet

It's morning breath
strong coffee, no cream
peanut butter and raspberry jam
cottage cheese with Lawry's season salt
mashed potatoes and gravy
graham crackers
a red cabernet

It's a mix of mower, chain saw, tractor, combine
grease and oil
fresh cut grass
millet, wheat, sorghum, sunflower
corn and crambe oil
It's the rolling of alfalfa and clover in his hands
soil not dirt

It's tea tree oil
a hint of Ivory or Irish Spring
his smooth clean skin
a splash of Brut or Old Spice
almond cherry lotion

unscented face cream

It's not just sweat and soil, tears and tea tree oil
it's his furry armpits and chest
fluids from a lifetime of lovemaking
the scent of us
my head resting upon his heart
his beating heart
the sound of his breath

I still have the last t-shirt he ever wore
the one he took off before he went to bed
the black one he took off on that Friday night
that July Friday night when the full moon was eclipsed
I see it puddled on the stained tan carpet
It's in the dark heart of my closet
I don't want it to fade

JULIE GARDNER, an Amherst Writers & Artists Affiliate and
Certified Life Legacies Facilitator, writes and leads writing groups and
retreats in Seattle and Bainbridge Island. She is the editor of *Original
Voices: Homeless and Formerly Homeless Women's Writings*. Grief, which
she defines as 'love in a different form', often shows up in her recent
writing.

SIBLING ESTRANGEMENT AND SOCIAL DISTANCING

By Caroline Leavitt

The words in the email punch my heart. "You're dead to me," my sister says. "I despise you. I hope you feel the pain that you keep causing me."

I do feel the pain. Her message has made me nearly hysterical because I don't understand how and why she could write something like that to me. Plus, it's now been a full month of corona, and the virus is raging on, and every connection anyone has matters more now. Or at least it is supposed to.

It wasn't always like this with us. Oh, no. We were close growing up, each other's best friend. She was beautiful, bright, and exotic, and I, the mousy shy one, used to bask in her light. And she let me, protecting me, encouraging me. We egged each other on, writing books together, wandering to Harvard Square to gawk at cute boys or shop for clothes we would both wear. We promised we would always live near each other, we would always keep each other's secrets, and when one needed the other, we would always be there. Later, she took me on her dates, sharing all of her life with me. We made up a code word for the one who died first to come back in spirit and whisper that word in the survivor's ear, so we would know we were still and always connected.

I can pinpoint when it started. I was seventeen and she was newly married, overwhelmed with a baby, and I was running wild, the way we used to do together and she no longer could. She'd snap at me or refuse to talk to me, and we'd see each other only when we both came home to visit our mother. With my mother as a buffer, we connected again. But those times didn't last, and as the years went on, I saw my sister less and less.

She finally told me, blurting it out, that she felt I had stolen her life, that I got the happy marriage and the writing career. I imagined that seeing me, being with me, reminded her of that and she had to protect herself against it. But we always, eventually, came back together, especially in crises that impacted us both. We moved my mom into independent living together. We took care of arrangements when my mom died, and I remember telling my sister that though our mom's death at one hundred was part of the natural order of things, if it had been my sister, I would have been devastated. I wouldn't have recovered from it. "Me, too, with you," she told me.

Except it wasn't true. She didn't want to talk on the phone or visit or have contact. If my presence couldn't bring her back to me, I reasoned that maybe material things could. Because I reviewed books, I had ARCs coming into my home every day. I cherry-picked the best ones and sent them to her, but she was miffed. She said I had sent her books that stunk. How could I think she would like this book or that? She posted on my social media about how she hated a book, and when I told her not to, that I was deeply protective of authors, she accused me of being a sycophant.

When I sent her a dress, it came back in the mail, with no note. When I sent her a necklace I'd had specially made for her, she tied it in knots and returned it to me with a scribbled note, "You like this. I don't."

And then one day, her daughter, now grown, reached out to me, and we became ridiculously close. I helped her with her writing and she helped me with mine; I doted on her young kids. Our two families loved each other. It was something I thought my sister might be happy about, and at first, she was. But then that changed. Her joy turned to fury, against me and against her daughter. She insisted that I cut contact with her daughter and her daughter's family altogether, because I was a bad influence, and because with me there, what room was there for her? When I told her I couldn't do that, a series of vitriolic emails spilled into my inbox. "Look at you," my husband said. "Your hands are shaking. You can't have contact."

But now there is COVID-19, and more than ever, I want contact. I'm still sure I can fix whatever has gone wrong between us. Just give me time, I think, but now, with the pandemic, there is no time. Contact with my sister is more important to me than ever. Except it's still not important to her.

"Why are you doing this?" my husband asks. "It's clear she thinks the relationship is over. And even if it wasn't, it isn't a healthy one. How can you be family with someone who's furious that you're happy? Someone who wants to hurt you?"

"She's unhappy," I tell him. "I hate it that she's unhappy."

I weep to my therapist on the phone. "She closed the door," my therapist calmly reminds me. And though she's right, I can't help trying to desperately pry the hinges open.

With COVID-19, I can't leave my city to travel to hers, to find her and make her see reason. I can't show up with flowers or books and beg her to talk to me. But there are things I can do at a social distance, things I've done before, and maybe this time they'll have more meaning.

She won't open any email with my name, so I get crafty and go to

AOL and open up a new account I call "Library News!" with an exclamation point so she'll open it. Inside it, I address her as a library reader that we, the libraries, will be thrilled to welcome back when we can. But in the meantime, perhaps she'd like to access some books online? Perhaps she'd like to use this IndieBound link to find and buy her favorite reads? Perhaps. Always perhaps. I have no idea if she follows through with anything I send, but it makes me happy to send things, to imagine that she does.

I want to know she's safe. I want to know she and her family members and her friends who mean something to her don't have the virus. And the truth is what I really yearn for. I want her to know that I am safe. I want her to still care about me, because for that not to be true feels unbearable, like a kind of death. It hurts, it hurts, it hurts.

"Give it up," my husband tells me. "Not everyone is going to love you. Family is biology, not an imperative."

Other women become sisters to me: a woman who totally gets what I am going through because her sibling will call to ask for something but insists she put the item in the mailbox so he doesn't actually see her. I make a friend who is so like me, I wonder if I grew up with her instead of my real sibling. It helps, but not totally.

Can't my sister love me now that a virus is decimating the planet? So much around me is being lost: people, places, a normal way of life. I can't bring those back, but can't I bring back our bond?

To calm myself, I begin to obsessively knit sweaters. I make one for myself, and then one for my sister's daughter, every stitch full of love and connection. I imagine making one for my sister, soft deep purple, a color she'd love, but I can't bear to think of her returning the sweater to me, of cutting the stitches the way she cut off our relationship.

So I go to my office and make up a new email address. I find links about how important it is to reach out, to forgive, to talk—especially now. I think about how making amends shouldn't have to be about taking abuse, how the world is changing but that doesn't mean people change or that their hearts soften. Sometimes they don't. My sister might always hate me, which is a strange and terrible thing. But I persist. I bait hooks, posting photos of her daughter, of her daughter's kids, on social media, everyone smiling and happy and inviting. I'm desperate for a response. I keep tweeting because I know she tracks my social media. I know this because she sometimes lashes out at me when she reads something she doesn't like. *My sister is estranged from me,* I post. I put up a broken heart emoji for good measure and I get about twenty responses from people who say: Me, too. But nothing from the one person it is meant for.

Sometimes, too, I imagine her reading this essay, her heart that is a fist loosening up, opening to my outstretched hand. I think that we might love each other again, that we might be sisters. And then I think about what it's like to not have the violence, the bitterness, the attacks, the astonishing relief if the broken drama of our relationship is not always playing out. It's then I feel the distance between us like the face mask I now wear, a protection that I might, or might not, need forever.

CAROLINE LEAVITT is the bestselling author of eleven novels, including *With or Without You*, and a book critic for the *San Francisco Chronicle* and other publications. She is cofounder of A Mighty Blaze and teaches writing online at Stanford and UCLA.

CELEBRATING IN THE PRESENT TENSE

By Meg Waite Clayton

My son defended his doctoral dissertation virtually this spring, from an apartment where he lives alone, 3,123 miles away from me. In normal times, one of his mentors would have brought a bottle of good champagne to toast the newly-minted Professor Clayton. In normal times, I'd have a ticket for a seat beside his eighty-seven-year-old grandfather on a six-hour flight to applaud the short moment Chris would walk across a stage in crimson silk gown and black-and-crimson hood with the white crow's-feet emblem of an economist.

Instead, we're looking for an alternative way to honor six years of incredibly hard work. I was caught without the eggs even to make his favorite flourless chocolate cake to mail to him, instead seeking advice by tweet about the possible name of that shop where he buys Thanksgiving pies. Could they deliver to his door in time for a pie to be quarantined, or would disinfecting the box with bleach spray be good enough?

Ceremony. Merriam-Webster defines it as "a formal act or series of acts prescribed by ritual, protocol, or convention." But what do you do when a pandemic makes ritual, protocol, and convention impossible? "Celebrate" is "to perform (a sacrament or solemn ceremony) publicly and with appropriate rites." Publicly.

It feels indulgent, to grieve such a small loss. My family remains alive and uninfected. We are not saying that last goodbye by phone to a loved one dying in a hospital room without our hand to hold. We are not postponing that last of life's ceremonies, the funeral.

And yet I cry in the shower, as do, I suppose, millions of us all over the world. We grieve the chance to celebrate those we love in what used to be the big moments in life, in the time before every moment of life itself seemed so big.

Moments that, for all of human history, have been marked by ceremony.

No flipping of tassels or tossing of graduation caps this May and June. Not for college students or PhDs. Not for high schools, middle schools, or preschools. Not for medical students, many of whom are already out working to defeat this virus. Even the U.S. Naval Academy, where the hat-tossing tradition began in 1912, tossed theirs this year without the benefit of an audience to applaud.

No dancing at weddings or comic stuffing of cake bites into newly-wed mouths. No babies crying over baptismal fonts. No awkward student welcomes and get-to-know-yous over the summer. Birthdays. Anniversaries. Publication parties. Film premieres. Retirements. Not even a Mother's Day brunch for most of us.

This spring, there will be none of those moments we photograph and paste into scrapbooks, share with our virtual friends, and set out in frames for years to come.

So we adapt. My niece introduces her new daughter to the family by Easter teleconference. My nephew considers delaying a fall wedding until we can all gather again. Zoom becomes a verb with a new meaning, and we have never been so grateful to be living in the time of video technology that was the stuff of TV make-believe when many of us were growing up.

My son, like so many graduates this year, will attend a virtual commencement and a "special online event" for some smaller group of

PhD candidates or economists, the details of which are being worked out now.

He will also be feted in person "sometime later, once we know it is safe to bring people together again," his university president assures us in an email, with "all of the pomp, circumstance, and tradition that is typical." We will be there, applauding all the more enthusiastically, appreciating these pivotal life moments even more somehow for having to experience them virtually, and to look forward to the time when "celebrate" is once again a present tense verb.

MEG WAITE CLAYTON is the bestselling author of seven novels, including *The Last Train to London, The Race for Paris,* and *The Wednesday Sisters.* Her work has been published in the *Los Angeles Times,* the *New York Times,* the *Washington Post, USA Today,* where this piece originally appeared, and many other publications.

MAYBE

By Anna Quinn

Maybe you're hurling curses at the purple crocuses and eating dinner at three o'clock because who can keep track of time anymore and dinner is mostly Doritos and pancakes, and you're afraid to drink that last carton of milk. The *use by* date has come and gone, but you keep checking the date, anyway.

Maybe you thought you were ready, and you weren't, you were born for this and you aren't, you were safe and you're not, and you mostly feel like a child hungry for milk and cookies and reassurance.

Maybe you're a single mom with three children and a mortgage and your Safeway shift begins at five a.m., and you've been wearing the same mask for a week and it's impossible to believe you'll survive this tremble of a time and to imagine what will happen to your children.

Maybe you ache of loneliness. Or maybe you're most alive in solitude. They're so different, loneliness and solitude, one is something missing, the other something found. Maybe you're between both spaces.

Maybe you've started a garden in your windowsill because it's hard not to hope when you plant seeds, or at least that's what you tell yourself, and then, you're inexplicably overwhelmed with happiness when the seeds burst through the surface and open their leaves to the sun.

Maybe you're making art and it's more fierce and tender than you imagined, or maybe you're not, because who can make art at a time like this.

Maybe you're noticing things need your attention and some of those things are huge like soul work, and some are mundane like cleaning the bathroom, and you're taking naps on the grass instead and imagining a stream flowing over you and you're too exhausted for epiphanies anyway.

Maybe your partner is taking chances that scare you. Maybe they don't think you're taking enough chances, and maybe you respond, But what if the next thing you touch kills you?

Maybe there are too many reminders that you're mortal, or some one is dying not in your arms or you're standing alone outside, looking in the window at your mother, the frightened blinks of her eyes, or the nurse is holding the phone to your sister's ear because she's on a ventilator but still you know she is listening because of the way she breathes.

Maybe you're not alone in your feelings and maybe you're holding space for someone, or someone is holding space for you, and maybe the most important things for those of us still here are subversive gestures of tenderness and courage and daring to touch the light.

ANNA QUINN is the author of *The Night Child*, (Blackstone, 2018). She is the cofounder of The Writers' Workshoppe and Imprint Bookstore in Port Townsend, Washington.

(*DAYENU*): DISPATCHES FROM THE COVID-19 SICK WARD

By Martha Anne Toll

The Week Before

Washington, DC, is beginning to shut down when our two adult daughters travel home—with difficulty—from Iowa and Boston.

Day 1

Second Daughter wakes up, does not feel well. Has shortness of breath and tightness in her chest. She's twenty-five and is otherwise (*Dayenu*)[1] in good health.

Our doctor says to isolate her immediately. "Lock her up, do the deepest clean possible, and leave food outside her door as needed."

Days 2-3

Second Daughter feels worse, more shortness of breath and tightness in her chest and back. Her health insurance (*Dayenu*, she has health insurance) is not permitted to authorize a test in this location. The local testing site declines her request; she doesn't tick off enough boxes (*Dayenu*, she isn't running a fever, doesn't have a persistent cough, and has no preexisting conditions).

Day 3

I feel lousy. I am short of breath, with strange itchy lungs. Like

---

1 "Dayenu" is a word recited during the Jewish Passover service that loosely translates as "gratitude," and more accurately as "it would have been sufficient" (*i.e.*, if only G-d had taken us out of Egypt, it would have been sufficient, but He also provided for us during forty years in the desert, etc.).

Second Daughter, I very rarely run a fever and do not now, but I have fever-like symptoms, sweats and chills.

By the afternoon, it dawns on me to try to get tested. I can tell that tomorrow I won't be able to get out of bed.

I set up an e-visit with my doctor who finds that due to my age (sixty-two) and other symptoms, I qualify for a test. A wonderful woman at Urgent Care takes my information, puts me in the queue, and says to come in. By now it's close to 5 p.m. Since neither of us thinks I have the energy to walk the two blocks there and back, my husband drives me. (*Dayenu*, I'm close to Urgent Care and have a husband/caretaker who can bring me.)

The wait is close to an hour and I stop outside where I can social distance. It's raw and windy, so I can't figure out why my husband is standing outside our car, talking on his phone.

He shouts from the street that the car battery has died right there, in front of Urgent Care. In my current stupor, I find this hysterically funny. This is also the day that the president announces his rollback of corporate average fuel economy (CAFE) standards. Those standards are the biggest single step any country has taken to fight global warming, and increasing CAFE standards has been my husband's lifework. His whole existence is turning into a macabre comedy.

I'm called back into Urgent Care, evaluated, and tested for flu, strep, and COVID-19. The first two are negative, but the COVID-19 results will take a week or more.

First Daughter has given our car a jumpstart and is there to take me home (*Dayenu*).

The Next Seven Days

I can't stay awake for more than one to two hours at a stretch. I'm short of breath. My lungs hurt, my trachea itches.

Second Daughter gets worse. Her back hurts where COVID-19 has found her lungs. She's had pneumonia before and thinks she's getting it again. She looks gray and peaked at all hours of the day. Her usual good humor has left her.

She gets teary. I'm anxious about her, but too sick to be my full-on worrying self.

The days pass in a hazy blur. Mostly I'm sleeping. Friends and family text the two healthy members of the household, offer help. They bring bagels and bread and gefilte fish for Passover (next week, an eternity away), homemade masks, and love. Amazing smells waft up from the kitchen where First Daughter cooks frittatas and curries and buttermilk biscuits (*Dayenu*). This, while she's still a full-time graduate student with teaching responsibilities.

At night, I turn into a werewolf. My husband has moved up to our attic (*Dayenu*, we have an attic). I wake up at 3:30 a.m., convinced this is it, my lungs are turning into rocks and it's time to go to the hospital to die. My ribs feel girdled and my breathing is short. It's too risky to wake my husband; it's unclear if I can make it up the steps to the attic or, for that matter, back down. I put on a mask and wake First Daughter. She's a wonderful comfort and good at breathing exercises. The on-call doctor reassures me that yes, I can sleep on my back without suffocating. If I can make it to the bathroom without getting short of breath, and still speak in sentences, I'm not ready for the hospital. He's proud I can walk in laps around my bed. He is the loveliest man I've ever spoken to.

Second Daughter's Boston doctor calls daily, and finally recommends antibiotics. They arrive within a day (*Dayenu*).

I'm ashamed to admit that I go through the identical routine the next night, except this time it's 4:30 a.m. and we don't bother the on-call doctor. First Daughter calms me down, tells me to go back to bed. I do!

My COVID-19 test comes back early. It's negative. Apparently some people test negative before they are in the full throes of the disease, at which point they would convert to positive. In my case, the medical establishment agrees that this itchy, hurty, epically fatiguing sucker is COVID-19.

Husband stops by every morning and noon to bring breakfast and lunch to Second Daughter and me. We drink a lot of tea. He cleans a lot of dishes and does a lot of handwashing.

Second Daughter gets a bump from her antibiotics but goes downhill the next day. One night I get a glimmer of what I used to feel like. I can concentrate for more than ten seconds.

The next morning, I'm unable to move. Too many things hurt, and breathing isn't great.

I'm crying more than I used to but I'm too tired to work into a real sob. I sleep all morning. I sleep all afternoon. I wake up, eat dinner, and watch *The Great British Baking Show* whenever I can stay up long enough to complete an episode.

It is the day before the first seder. Usually we host twenty-five people—I would have cooked for weeks, taken days preparing ritual foods. I'm so tired, I can't give it a moment's thought.

First Daughter makes it happen. I coach her on the broth for matzo ball soup. There's a huge eggplant parmesan in the freezer, and there's just enough matzo meal left from last year to make matzo balls (*Dayenu*).

It's warm enough that we can be on the deck (*Dayenu*, we have a deck). Second Daughter and I can stay masked and keep enough distance to listen into a Zoom seder with cousins in DC, New York, and Florida.

The next morning, Second Daughter and I feel better, which turns out to be a false positive.

The Next Several Weeks

Seven weeks in, we remain in slow motion, winded by a walk around the block.

We know our cases are mild. We know we are lucky beyond measure to have a loving family, a comfortable place to recover, healthcare, and food. (*Dayenu*.)

The world is hurting and breaking. The present contains a level of suffering impossible to grasp. In the dim, uncertain future, we can hope healthcare and comfort won't depend on luck. We can hope humaneness, kindness, and truth are norms.

MARTHA ANNE TOLL's essays and reviews appear regularly in *NPR Books*, *The Millions*, and the *Washington Post*, and her fiction in a range of publications. She is the founding executive director of the Butler Family Fund, a philanthropic organization.

QUARANTINE

By Susan Henderson

Masks

My mom and I sit six feet apart in the living room of my child-hood home, both of us in masks and gloves. My father died last night, and I drove from New York to northern Virginia to be with her. While she cries, I sit here on the other side of the room, feeling my own breath against my face. It's an awful way to grieve. For fourteen days I can't hug her. Worse is knowing, since my father died, *no one* has hugged her.

Shiver

He'd been healthy until only recently. We traveled together last summer. He'd buzz my hotel room at five in the morning to see if I was up for a walk. A month ago, my mom called to say, "He's stopped eating. He doesn't want you to come, but I think you should."

When I arrived, I found him in the recliner, shivering under a blanket and heating pad. She didn't tell him I was coming. He hadn't shaved or combed his hair.

Papers

I came here to grieve with my mother, but we haven't had time. There are policy numbers to find, military discharge papers to send, passwords to guess. I'm cranky, reading forms I don't understand.

Swallow

I wanted my dad to have an appetite again. I thought if he ate more protein, more fat, he might rally. I didn't know his belly was full of cancer. I made a list of what I planned to feed him, aiming for two thousand calories a day. Next to that list, I wrote the foods that actually went into his mouth: one bite of pear, two sips of Ensure, one spoonful of scrambled eggs. I tallied the day's calories as we watched the world collapse each night on the news. On the day a cluster of COVID-19 cases appeared in my beloved New York, my father ate 120 calories. When Italy went on lockdown, he ate 310. The day the stock market hit a record low, he ate close to a thousand calories but I had to subtract for vomit and diarrhea.

Obituary

This is one of my favorite memories of my dad. My kids, eight and ten at the time, talked him into digging a moat in our yard. They spent the whole day shoveling and making a drawbridge, none of us remembering that the cesspool was buried in that same spot. I'm trying to write my dad's obituary, and this is one of many stories I cut to stay within our budget.

Listen

From my childhood bedroom, I listened for something awful to happen. One night he woke up sweating and confused. Another, he didn't make it to the bathroom in time. I scrubbed the floor and walls at 3 a.m., sorry he could hear me cleaning up after him.

Flag

I drive my dad's car to the funeral home to pick up his ashes and the folded flag they give to military servicemen. It's raining, and I can't find the switch for the wipers. At the funeral home, I stand, dripping on the carpet. All of us wear masks. They set a bag on the table. My father. When they step away, I'm allowed to approach.

I'm surprised by the sense of relief that he's with me again, that I'm taking him home. Rain thumps the roof as I pull off the highway. I stop for a long time in the Pentagon parking lot, where he taught me to drive. Sometimes I'm fine. Sometimes I weep with no sound.

Next sunny day, the boy across the street stands at the end of our walkway and plays a Bach sonata on his violin. My mom sits on the steps in her mask, with only the flag to hug.

Dare

One day, he did not get up at all. He lay on his back, looking at the ceiling. He declined my offers to turn on a radio, to read him the newspaper. He took only three sips of water, never used the bathroom. At night, his room dark again, I took a chance at something new. "I love you, Dad." He said it back to me, his first time too. In my room, I wondered if he'd die in the night, if my mom was holding him or if he would die alone.

Cans

The neighbors wheel their recycling cans to the curb and point the handles toward the road. Our can is filled with bottles of Ensure and unread newspapers. I assume the virus is on the trash cans, the mail, the door handle. I wash my hands, but have I been careful enough?

Turn

The virus spread through New York and the homes of my friends and

103

neighbors. It looked as if my state might follow Italy and go on lockdown. I told my father as I helped him sit up in bed. He was too weak to move his blanket aside. His legs were stained from diarrhea. "Here, eat something," I begged him. I'd mixed ice cream with Ensure, but he could not grip the spoon. I fed him one bite at a time. When he turned his face toward the wall, I pretended not to see his tears.

Teeth

I find a box of my baby teeth. They are taped to the bottom and numbered in the order I lost them. I'm falling apart. But unlike my father, who suffered quietly, I rant and slam doors.

Choose

When I reminded my dad to take another sip of Ensure, he snapped, "Don't tell me when to eat!" I felt complicit in his starvation. I stormed into the woods behind my elementary school and called my husband, sobbing into the phone.

"I think you should come home," he said.

"What if I miss my dad's last days?"

"What if they lock down New York and you can't get home?"

Rock

I sit in the woods by the creek and a mask floats by. I find a pile of painted rocks on a tree stump. A note says you can take one or leave one. I take one for my dad.

Wave

My husband drove down to Virginia to get me so I wouldn't have to travel through Penn Station. In case he was a carrier of the virus, he'd only say hello from the lawn. My dad struggled for balance as my mom dressed him. He took baby steps, panting, holding the wall. He stood behind the storm door and waved, the last we'd see him.

Music

I cry easily these days—ask the poor receptionists at the Pentagon Federal Credit Union and Dominion Energy—but there are signs we'll be okay. My mother has begun to reimagine her life going forward. She thinks the room where we watch TV could become an art studio. She's unpacked her guitar—it's been decades—and keeps it propped beside the couch. During my shower, I blast Earth, Wind & Fire and discover I can still feel joy.

Salute

My dad weighed one hundred pounds when he died. Those last days I spent with him were brutal, tender, an honor.

Masks

All I desire anymore are simple things: to be out in the world without a mask, to pet a stranger's dog, to sit close enough to the people I love to hear them breathe. I walk past my elementary school, empty now, and slip into the woods behind it once again. That last image of my father sits like a weight in my chest. I take every trail until the exertion reminds me to let in air. I step off the path to make room for a woman with a bandana tied around her face. We are connected—all of us with our smiles and sorrows hidden from each other, all of us so in need of human touch. As the woman continues on her walk, I check my phone. I've been here longer than I planned. I turn back toward the house, and start to run out of the woods and through my childhood streets. For fourteen days, no one has hugged my mom, but our quarantine is finally over. I hurry and, reaching for the door, have already flung off my mask.

SUSAN HENDERSON is the author of *The Flicker of Old Dreams* and *Up from the Blue*, both published by HarperCollins. She's a lifetime member of the National Book Critics Circle and the NAACP.

NOT THE SADDEST THING IN THE WORLD

By Ada Limón

All day I feel some itchiness around
the collar, constriction of living. I write

the date at the top of a letter, though
no one has been writing the year lately

I write the year, seems like a year you
should write, huge and round and awful.

In between my tasks, I find a dead fledgling,
maybe dove, maybe dunno to be honest,

too embryonic, too see-through and wee.
I don't even mourn him, just all matter-of-

fact-like take the trowel, plant the limp body
with a new hosta under the main feeder.

Seems like a good place for a closed-eyed
thing, forever closed-eyed, under a green plant

in the ground, under the feast up above. Between
the ground and the feast is where I live now.

Before I bury him, I snap a photo and beg
my brother and my husband to witness this

nearly clear body. Once it has been witnessed
and buried, I go about my day which isn't

ordinary exactly because nothing is ordinary
now even when it is ordinary. Now, something's

breaking always on the skyline falling over
and over against the ground sometimes

unnoticed, sometimes covered up like sorrow,
sometimes buried without even a song.

ADA LIMÓN is the award-winning author of five books of poetry,
including *The Carrying* and *Bright Dead Things*. She serves on the
faculty of Queens University of Charlotte Low-Residency MFA
program and Provincetown Fine Arts Work Center, and works as a
freelance writer in Lexington, Kentucky.

PART THREE: COMFORT

IN CONVERSATION WITH
DANI SHAPIRO

"We need to pay attention to what's happening at this very moment."

Dani Shapiro has a talent for making sense of the shifting landscape of identity during times of crisis, as she has demonstrated in five bestselling memoirs. *Devotion* is a poignant examination of faith while struggling with the early loss of her father, a troubled relationship with her mother, and her infant son's life-threatening illness. Her latest memoir, *Inheritance*, details her quest to uncover the true meaning of identity and family after discovering the father she grew up with is not her biological father. Her new podcast, *The Way We Live Now*, examines the way people from all walks of life are coping during the COVID-19 pandemic. I've interviewed Dani numerous times during the past decade, and I knew she would have wise words about finding comfort and meaning during this troubled time.

Jennifer Haupt: How are you finding meaning during the pandemic? And how do we get back to normal?

Dani Shapiro: One thought I've been having is that the pandemic is happening to ALL of us. There is no one on the planet who is not being affected by this disaster, which is unlike anything we've experienced in our lifetime—maybe ever in history. The meaning comes in the knowledge that we are dependent on our interconnectedness if we are to go back to some kind of normalcy—not as we know it before the pandemic, but some kind of robust living.

JH: We are more interconnected in some ways: Seth Meyers telling jokes from his living room, with his books in the background instead of the Rockefeller Plaza studio. Trevor Noah commiserating with us nightly about his shelter-in-place boredom. Governor Cuomo's voice cracking during a recent interview, talking about his brother being ill with COVID-19.

DS: Yes, the blurring of space between our public and private selves is happening in all sorts of ways. People are hungrier than ever for connections. It's a big part of self-care.

JH: What do you see as the biggest challenge, in terms of emotional self-care?

DS: Managing fear, for sure. How we process the instability, the constantly shifting terror that has invaded our lives, is critical. We need to do what we can to maintain whatever control we do have over our lives.

For example, when the shelter-in-place order hit Connecticut, where I live, I had been on book tour for a year. My world was about how I'd manage to get from one place to another, nearly every day. And then, quite suddenly, I went from that constant movement to having blank pages in my calendar. The plans that had been the tent poles for my illusion of control were pulled right out of the ground. I had to make new plans, live by new rules, which took some doing.

JH: What did that new plan look like for you?

DS: I started a second podcast, *The Way We Live Now*, interviewing people from all walks of life—from a grocery store manager, to doctors and nurses, to a mobile dog groomer, to a biochemist—about their experiences of the pandemic. In part, I wanted to process what life is like for all of us. And, in large part, I was looking for a new way to connect with people—meeting readers person-to-person at bookstores was obviously not going to happen for quite some time.

JH: What have you learned from interviewing people on the front lines of the pandemic, about how they are taking care of themselves?

DS: What strikes me most is that they don't want to be called heroes. Helping others, interacting with others, is part of their identity. For example, I interviewed a doctor, Suzanne, who's over age sixty. She received an email asking if she'd do COVID-19 screening at the hospital where she worked. Her first gut response, out of fear, was "No way." She dragged the email into the trash. But then, two days later, she fished it out. She realized she could no more not go than fly. Once she was working in the unit, where she was most needed, her fear went away.

JH: I've heard everyone say the same thing, from store clerks, to my pharmacist, to a friend who's a physical therapist. The gratitude they receive from others feeds their souls. The connections are a great comfort during this time of isolation.

DS: A piece of it has to do with identity. The sense that this is my life, this is my role. If I don't do this, I wouldn't be me. Standing firmly in one's self mitigates some of the fear of putting oneself at risk of getting the disease.

JH: Even those of us not on the front lines are living in such immense, constant fear. It's overwhelming. How do we manage to stay calm and focused?

DS: Fear makes us want to run: fight or flight. We think we can run from the discomfort, but in fact, sitting still and noticing discomfort as a feeling state—not as a reality—is what helps most. Meditation, which can be as simple as sitting in a quiet, comfortable space, grounds you in the present moment.

For most of us, unless we are on the front lines, the present moment does not actually hold anything to be afraid of. I know if I wake up and meditate for twenty minutes, I feel better because I'm not leaning into the future—that's where a lot of fear comes from. The thing about meditation is that it really does train us to come back to the present moment. What's happening at this very moment is that I'm breathing in, I'm breathing out. You may have to do that fifty times a day, for a few minutes each time, because the mind isn't going to easily fall in line with that, but we have lots of time now to train ourselves.

DANI SHAPIRO is the author of five memoirs, most recently the *New York Times* bestseller *Inheritance*, as well as five novels, including *Black & White* and *Family History*. She teaches writing workshops all over the world and lives with her family in Litchfield County, Connecticut.

TODAY, WHEN I COULD DO NOTHING

By Jane Hirshfield

Today, when I could do nothing,
I saved an ant.

It must have come in with the morning paper,
still being delivered
to those who shelter in place.

A morning paper is still an essential service.

I am not an essential service.

I have coffee and books,
time,
a garden,
silence enough to fill cisterns.

It must have first walked
the morning paper, as if loosened ink
taking the shape of an ant.

Then across the laptop computer—warm—
then onto the back of a cushion.

Small black ant, alone,
crossing a navy cushion,
moving steadily because that is what it could do.

Set outside in the sun,
it could not have found again its nest.
What then did I save?

It did not look as if it was frightened,
even while walking my hand,
which moved it through swiftness and air.

Ant, alone, without companions,
whose ant-heart I could not fathom—
how is your life, I wanted to ask.

I lifted it, took it outside.

This first day when I could do nothing,
contribute nothing
beyond staying distant from my own kind,
I did this.

JANE HIRSHFIELD's most recent, ninth book of poetry is *Ledger*. Also the author of two now-classic books of essays and four books collecting the work of world poets of the deep past, Hirshfield was elected in 2019 into the American Academy of Arts & Sciences.

THREE O'CLOCK

By Jennie Shortridge

What do you do when there's nothing you can do, no matter how actively the fight-or-flight center in your brain wants you to do something? *Anything.*

I'm sixty years old and immune compromised. For the hat trick, I live with anxiety disorder, no small challenge in a pandemic. On the plus side, my husband and I haven't lost our work or income. Anything we need can be delivered. Our lifestyle hasn't even changed much; we've worked from home for years. But my amygdala doesn't care that I'm physically safe. That almond-shaped nut in the center of my brain shoots a steady stream of alarms into my nervous system: *Run for your life! No, wait, fight! No, shit . . . run?*

Days into Seattle's January outbreak I began to wake up reliably at three a.m. to freak out. No stranger to insomnia, I know how to calm myself. I take a long breath and imagine the word "thirty." After a slow exhalation, I take another breath, think "twenty-nine," and continue. If I'm still awake by zero, I list things I'm grateful for.

Now, of course, I begin with listing my safety, my husband's, my family's . . . well, no, that's not true anymore. My cousin just passed away in an East Coast care facility from COVID-19. My sister, a nurse in an Atlanta hospital, wears the same N95 mask she's worn since the outbreak began. And my octogenarian dad was barely out of the hospital when coronavirus struck, and the near miss isn't comforting.

All I can do now is ask for help from some loving entity, but my amygdala's having none of it.

For God's sake, do *something!* it shouts, pumping adrenaline through my body.

I breathe, count my blessings, pray, and hope for a little grace, along with some rest.

———

I had trouble getting to sleep from the get-go. My mother sang lullabies at bedtime, but my eyes stayed wide, my brow furrowed. Mom switched to telling stories, but these were no bedtime fare.

"The Sandman visits little children who are still awake," she said, "and sprinkles sand in their eyes to make them feel sleepy. Don't worry, honey, he'll be here soon."

"But how does he get into our house?" My chin trembled.

"He's magic, like Santa."

"But I don't want him to come."

"Just relax," she said, kissing my head, her essence of Jergens lotion and cigarette smoke blanketing me. "Close your eyes, now, and go to sleep."

Maybe she was riffing on "Mr. Sandman," a pretty radio hit the year she met Dad. I only knew one appropriate response—stay awake and fight off the monster. Who wanted sand in their eyes? How would that make you sleepy, anyway, and not just in agony?

And who needed another monster roaming the dark late at night, long after the house had gone quiet? We already had one.

———

During week two of the shutdown, a new foe enters my life: three o'clock in the afternoon. Each day, as my work concentration peters out, a wave of nausea swells inside me. It begins with me doing the worst thing—reading the scariest news about COVID-19. My first inclination when in danger has always been to learn everything I can about the problem. She who keeps her eyes open to trouble and understands it survives, according to four-year-old me, and it can work with issues less virulent than a killer virus. I gain some semblance of control.

With each report of the worsening outbreak, though, I grow lightheaded from shallow breathing. My gag reflex threatens. My stomach roils, wanting to spew every frightening thing I've ingested, every ghost of memory and terror. The existential threat I sensed in childhood is writ large, now, and frighteningly real.

These are indicators that I'm literally making myself sick with worry. It's a reflex similar to fainting at the sight of blood, where the trigger of extreme distress causes the heart rate and blood pressure to plummet, and down you go.

This is the opposite of being in control.

———

As a young adult in therapy, I learned that my childhood monsters were born of Mom's tempestuous mental disorders. There were the monsters she told stories about, like the Sandman, or the peeping Toms she said were outside our windows. There were ghosts, including a poltergeist she claimed lived in my bedroom. And there was that monster we never talked about: my mom, lurking in the dark hours, too manic, too depressed, or too delusional to sleep.

I became hardwired with fear and panic. In some ways, that saved me as a kid. I sensed Mom's moods and learned to disappear as needed by staying quiet, being "good," blending in with the curtains.

That hardwiring proves helpful now, too. My need to figure out everyone and everything and fix it all found a rewarding outlet when

I became a novelist. Now, exerting control over a cast of characters in untenable situations is something I do for joy. But some of my fight-or-flight reactions can also knock me out of sync with reality. Hypervigilance (or "research," as I like to call it) isn't a panacea for staying safe; it's a symptom of feeling unsafe, just like shallow breathing, muscle clenching, perseverating, not sleeping, and yes, feeling about to puke.

The hard truth is that no one has control over what will happen in any given moment, only over how we react. And in this pandemic that will be my—and our—saving grace.

———

It's week who-knows-what-anymore and I'm limiting myself to one read of the headlines each day and maybe a deeper read of what's happening with remedies, vaccines, and other useful information. I accompany that with conscious, relaxed breathing. I ignore the scary stories, even though I'm drawn to them.

We can stay physically safe from coronavirus with social distancing and protective gear. We can also manage the overwhelming fear of it by limiting stimuli and practicing mindfulness until the discomfort subsides. And because this threat isn't going away anytime soon, we can resolve to keep doing these things for as long as it takes.

I have a proactive relationship with three a.m. and three p.m. now. I unclench my jaw and hands, let cool air into my lungs and warm air out. I am changing. Everything is changing, because it must.

Jennie Shortridge is the author of *Love Water Memory* and other bestselling novels. She is currently at work on a memoir about her mother.

ALONE AND AWASH IN DESIRE

By Sonora Jha

So come to the pond,
or the river of your imagination,
or the harbor of your longing,
and put your lips to the world.

And live
your life.
    — Mary Oliver, "Red Bird"

The first thing she feels is relief. This thing hasn't caught her off-guard at all. She knows how to stay home all alone. She's done it before. She's even written about it and put it out there. The world knows she can be alone. The world won't come around knocking.

She's lived alone for almost a year some years ago. And back then, she was crying from walking out on her second marriage.

This time, there is nothing to cry about. Nothing, of course, but for a pandemic and death all around. But the tears won't come.

So, the next thing she must feel is fear. She could fall sick and die alone. She reads the papers and learns that people are dying alone. People with families. People who live with six other people, loved by all six, are dying alone.

Don't let me die alone, she texts her son. Yes, she will burden him. He is twenty-four and has just moved to Boston to be a software engineer. She *must* burden him.

Don't go outside, he texts her back. Please don't go outside.

She makes a list. She buys fresh and frozen and canned things. The spinach and the ice cream. She goes online and orders Indian treats—*gulab jamun, rasgulla, Bikaneri sev.* They don't know yet, on the news, whether death will roll in like a hurricane or will settle in like a fog. If she senses death coming, she will eat the Indian treats first.

On her list, she writes down: Man. She inserts: White. A white man would come in handy if the supremacists settle in like a fog. She texts a man, a friend, with whom she recently had a sort of falling out. A pandemic is a shitty time to be fighting, she says. He responds right away: I'm glad you wrote. They make macabre jokes and she feels better. Come get me if shit goes down, she tells him. They talk about horror films.

The world is divided between those who haven't and those who have watched horror films and know how shit goes down with zombies or after the apocalypse. The world is divided between those who trust white people and those who don't, and she doesn't know which one she is.

To her Indian friends on Zoom, she says: Now I know why people stay married. They all laugh. Each one of them has a husband. Six weeks later, two of them will text to say they wish they didn't have husbands. She knows they will feel differently the week after.

The last time she was alone, she was still a mother who could fail her child. Now, she has no one to fail. She makes her bed and cleans up clutter and her small home is beautiful. A month goes by. She must still show up for Zoom meetings and is running a course for her students online, but there are no friends to be met with to hold their fears. No gym in which to sweat out the pounds of being a woman. No hours and hours of performing womanhood.

She has never done this, this barest minimum of things.

In the days of silence shorn of time, she plays with her dog, stares at the bridge and the lake outside her window, and reads nothing. She misses no one, not even her son. The most shameful thing—she wakes up with a spring in her step because, for the first time in her life, she must do nothing at all. Really. She could vanish into the walls and no one would see her disappearing shape or hear what happened.

If a tree falls in a forest . . . If a woman lives by herself, did she really live or may she die?

More people die, so she uses Amazon Prime to order a shit-ton of incense. She's going to pray her way out of this. It will be okay, because she's praying for the whole world, so it's all right to embrace her Hindu deities. She will dance in her condo's living room. She will build her own fog and inhale and weep from the assault on her sense of smell. She will burn *naag champa* and sway like the cobra that lives on the edge of a forest but not too far from a village with a source of water.

Have you ever stood in front of a mirror and tried to love your self? She used to love telling the men who loved her that she woke up every morning and looked in the mirror and found that she had become more beautiful than the previous day. They loved hearing that stuff. Men love women who believe they are beautiful. They don't like arrogant women, though. Her statement might have seemed arrogant, except she was speaking of beauty and she said it just shyly enough, and all of this pleased them until she sent them away.

Somewhere in the past year, she has stopped waking up more beautiful each day. Something has shifted in her face and she sees age flicker between her brows then dive down to the two crevices on the sides of her mouth.

I don't see it, her kind BFF says to her on Zoom.

She does not know why she is not panicked about age. In the silence and the silence and the silence, she loses her hold on panic, on despair, on misery.

She sits down to make a list of what she wants after the pandemic ("after this thing is over," people have started to say). Nothing comes.

She has emptied her head of information and she cannot even replace it with imagination.

She laughs so hard that the dog is startled and scampers into the other room.

But she has *always* wanted something. Don't take that away from me, she says to the house plant.

Her fifty-second birthday comes and goes. On her fiftieth, she'd told her son that she had lived all her dreams and had nothing, really, on her bucket list. I have traveled, I have been married twice, been loved and loved back. I have been a professional and a mother. I have survived disease and displacement. So, if I die now, just know that I lived a fulfilled life, she'd said to her child.

Okay, cool, but it would be nice if you didn't die, he'd said.

More people die. She lives more days, for no reason at all. A *New York Times* news alert appears on her phone: "*Like someone injected you with straight up fire." A teen's heart failure is a stark example of a new affliction in children tied to the coronavirus.*

She longs for her students. She longs for their language. Straight-up fire.

And slowly she is awash in a desire for her own life, some of it lived and some yet unlived. More, she whispers to her slippers. More.

She is hungry. She smells of cake from longing. She screams out song after song. She prays into scented smoke for the best love of her life to come along. Ten weeks and a hundred thousand deaths later, she opens her front door to a virtual stranger and falls into his arms.

On the morning of that day, though, she puts the kettle on. She watches the tea darken the water in her favorite china cup. She tortures her index finger with the steam. She raises the gold rim of the cup to her lips, sniffs the sweet bergamot, and kisses what may be the last thing she can control.

Sonora Jha is the author of the novel *Foreign*. She is a journalism professor at Seattle University. Her collection of linked essays titled *How to Raise a Feminist Son: Motherhood, Masculinity, and the Making of a Family*, comes out from Sasquatch Books in April 2021.

APEX GAZING
A RECORD OF MARCH 2020
By Lena Khalaf Tuffaha

It was the time of late empire,
and science and song
were all the rage. Chart after nightly chart
were rushed to the screen. Hieroglyphs
better left undeciphered. The news reports
a forecast of the magnitude of impending losses,
how late we were
arriving at our great battle.

It was the time of loud lies
and we baked until the stores ran out of flour;
our cookies delectable with a dusting of cinnamon
to warm the tongue, our butter browned, our sugar
raw, indelicate.

It was the time of virtual gatherings
and together we named the flowering street trees
beyond our windows. *Prunus spinosa* that erupted
in flowers like globes of snow, *Prunus serrulata* that canopied
our cautious strolls. Our distant loved ones were closer
and more unreachable as the largest birds
of our era lay dormant in our airports.
They sent photographs of their trees, too. *Tilia cordata*
of childhood memory, *Jacaranda mimosifolia*
not yet bloomed, a symphony on the verge.

It was the time of best case scenarios
and we tracked and catalogued, each of us
drafting a field guide for the terra nullius
that awaited us. *Stay home Stay home*
Melospiza melodia chirped
with singular clarity. *Cyanocitta stelleri*
rustled through evergreens in azulene flashes,
a choir, discordant,
in the silence of cities ailing
and freeways shorn of their gridlock.

It was the time of paltry metaphors,
and even the believers among us
soured at the prospect of April miracles.
Our grief gusted and down-poured, vernal
restlessness swelling each day beneath our roofs.

It was the time of superlatives,
and we languished. Postponements cluttered
our calendars. Between fears and stretching
we alternated, child and parent, bewildered.
We wiped down every surface, renewed in our frailty.

LENA KHALAF TUFFAHA is a poet, essayist, and translator.
Her first book of poems, *Water & Salt* (Red Hen Press) won the
2018 Washington State Book Award. She is also the author of two
chapbooks, *Arab in Newsland* (Two Sylvias Press, 2016) and *Letters
from the Interior* (Diode Editions, 2019).

IN THE BATHTUB

By Jenna Blum

The worst day I had during the pandemic took me by surprise. It wasn't the day I heard the virus might last eighteen months or the day I spent stocking canned goods to prepare for the breakdown of civilization. It wasn't anything close to what my doctor and nurse friends were experiencing. It was an ordinary day on which nothing really terrible had happened to me—ordinary in the COVID sense, which means not really ordinary at all.

It was 5 p.m. on a Tuesday—pub day on A Mighty Blaze, the social media platform Caroline Leavitt and I cofounded, along with eighteen volunteers, to connect quarantined writers with readers. Tuesdays were hectic because new books drop that day, and I'd been working at my dining room table in my underwear, glasses, and messy bun, looking forward to my evening walk with my friend Kirsten. She texted me as I was wrapping up: *Don't go out—there's a shooter on the Common.*

Kirsten lived on one side of the Boston Common and I on the other, and we met often for socially distanced strolls, each other's in-person connection. Missing one walk shouldn't have been a big deal, but when I got that text I slammed my iPad closed.

I wanted to go outside. I wanted exercise. I wanted nature. I needed that one excursion into open air.

The previous day, Kirsten hadn't been available and I'd walked anyway. The magnolias were blooming on Commonwealth Avenue, heavier and more lustrous than I could remember. Mother Nature was happy with the pandemic, fewer people driving and flying, the air clear over China, dolphins swimming through Venetian canals. Spring, at least, was unstoppable. I'd lifted my face to the blossoms and inhaled, but I could barely catch the scent through my mask.

Now I was done. Done having to enjoy flowers through a filter. Done being unable to walk. Done with the Blaze. I wanted to write. I wanted the gym. I wanted my friends. I wanted my dog, who'd died a few months before. I wanted my mom, who'd died a year before that. I wanted there not to be a shooter.

At that particular moment, my friend Stephen called. "Checking in, my dear," he said. "How are you?" Stephen knew how worried I was, thanks to reading Stephen King's *The Stand* and Emily St. John Mandel's *Station Eleven*, that there'd be a complete social breakdown. He'd assured me this wouldn't happen but that if it did, I'd be welcome at his rural Vermont home, to which I'd already invited myself.

"Honestly? I'm bad," I said. "I'm done with COVID, I'm done with the whole fucking thing."

"Have you eaten today?" he asked.

"NO," I said. I went to the refrigerator and opened it, then slammed it closed. "I don't WANT to eat."

"Have you showered?"

"Of COURSE not," I said.

"All right, here's what I want you to do," Stephen said. "Go run a bath. I'll even try hard not to imagine you naked."

I was in such bad shape I didn't even banter back. "FINE," I said, once I'd stripped and the water was running. "I'm in the tub."

"Good," he said. "Now I'm going to read you some poetry."

"I DON'T WANT ANY FUCKING POETRY," I said. "I just want my LIFE BACK!"

"I understand," Stephen said. "Now: listen."

I sat in the tub with Stephen on speaker, scowling as he read me poem after poem. I couldn't concentrate. The words slid off me. They meant nothing. But I didn't hang up. I let Stephen's voice wash over me. I lay back and shut my eyes.

"Better?" asked Stephen. I grunted.

"Not yet, apparently," he said. "Let's try this one."

For an hour he read as I lay with the water cooling. Eventually, I was able to bite down on what he was reading, my brain starting to make sense of the words. It was like a picture coming into focus, only the picture was myself. I sighed.

"Better?" Stephen asked.

"Yes," I said. "Thank you."

"It's my privilege," he said. "Will you be all right?"

"Now I will," I said. "Stephen?"

"Yes?"

"That last one was yours, wasn't it," I said.

"Good ear, my dear," he said. I smiled. The last poem was the first one I'd been truly able to hear.

These Nights of Candles By Stephen P. Kiernan

The old man raises his cane
and fences with the swords of gladiolus.
He's frenzied in the garden. The sun inches west
and on its last red edge
matches are being struck, lighters thumbed,
the candles begin

though some people are already asleep:
the postman, his fingers inked by commerce
and wordy romance, not one promise or plea
written to him; the early rising baker,
a bachelor till his last baguette;
the fisherman, whose wife stands at the window
staring at a sea that contains nothing
but her vague reflection on the glass.
And the butcher's wife, reluctantly, lies down
for her heavy husband, and after a time
feels like meat pounded on the gristle.
The preacher sips red before a blank page
certain the sermon will appear whole
once he finds the first word,
while the silence of the house presses down.
Nearby the drunkard prepares his singing voice
and wonders who did this to his hands.
The old man is led to his room and left there.

These nights of candles, these heartbreaks burned low,
are not the only kind. Somewhere, someone
is making a toast to ten friends, some man
is kissing a woman's belly and she's laughing.
A baby under blankets breathes
like the moon's phases, like falling snow.
Some candles light a page or a window
or a church or a birth
or a friend's or a lover's face.

But tonight, like most nights, when I cup my hand
behind the flame, when it highlights

every whorl and ridge and fortune teller's line
and I breathe in, I know I am about to lose you forever
again, and no kind of light can save me,
and I cannot help breathing out.
There's a brief glow in the wick's tip,
but then the smoke. The old man
sits a hard chair and remembers.
Down in the street a moonbright hound
howls and howls and howls.

JENNA BLUM is the internationally bestselling author of the novels *Those Who Save Us*, *The Stormchasers*, and *The Lost Family*, and one of Oprah's Top 30 Women Writers. Based in Boston, Jenna is cofounder of A Mighty Blaze and a twenty-year teacher at GrubStreet.

STEPHEN P. KIERNAN is the author of *The Curiosity*, *The Baker's Secret*, *The Hummingbird*, and *Universe of Two* (August 2020). A career journalist, Stephen has also written two nonfiction books, *Last Rights* and *Authentic Patriotism*.

SEARCHING FOR GRACE
DURING LOCKDOWN

By Jean Kwok

Living with joy, even if imperfectly, is a kind of salvation.

My mother, a kind and generous soul, was a perfectionist when it came to the definition of a good Chinese daughter. Dumpling wrappers were rolled out to perfectly uniform thickness, then cut and pleated around the finely chopped filling. Woks weren't clean unless they were scrubbed with steel wool. The water for cooking rice needed to be exactly deep enough to cover the first segment of your index finger when you touched a fingertip to the surface of the raw rice.

"But, Ma," I would ask, "what if someone has freakishly long fingers, like Cousin Wu? Or what if the pot is tall and thin instead of—" I'd break off at the sight of her narrowed eyes. My mother often warned me that if I didn't shape up, there would be consequences. Now that my husband and two sons are cooped up with me in CO-VID-19 lockdown, I understand what she meant.

Our family had been quite wealthy in China, but over the course of our immigration to the United States, we lost everything. At five years old, I found myself living in an unheated, roach-infested apartment in the slums of Brooklyn. After school each day, my father would bring me to the sweatshop in Chinatown to help work as best I could.

Despite the rats that crept alongside our mattresses every night, my old-fashioned mother maintained her dignity and her standards, especially regarding her youngest daughter's behavior. Anything that might have helped me learn any degree of athleticism was considered unladylike and therefore forbidden: skipping, running, turning cartwheels. Furthermore, there was no time or money for any extra-curricular activity that might have nourished coordination, like ballet or swimming. My friends at school giggled over their dance recitals and new tutus while I listened with envy and admiration. And finally, worst of all, I was a dreamy, impractical child, a hopeless combination of cluelessness and curiosity.

I melted the plastic handle of one of my mother's cherished pots while boiling water because I forgot to keep an eye on the flames. I secretly took apart my father's radio to see how it worked—I was planning to put it back together, really—and was caught on our worn vinyl floor, surrounded by tiny screws and parts. Glasses and bowls slipped out of my hands as if they had been greased. My family would call me repeatedly to sweep the floor, only to find me staring out the window, dreaming of other lives and worlds. As a Chinese daughter, I was an unmitigated disaster.

In some ways, school wasn't much better. After I learned English, my talent for learning kicked in and my classmates started calling me the "Queen of the Brains." This was no help in gym, where my gym teacher yelled at me to climb the rope hanging from the ceiling while I stared at him as if he were insane. I was also nearsighted, yet nothing could convince me to wear my huge purple glasses. (Despite my ill-fitting clothing and frizzy hair, I still had a bit of vanity left.) The result was that any ball headed in my direction was a blur at best, and I'd simply try to avoid it. However, I was good at all of the other subjects, so I experienced that duality of being considered a success in the outside world and an utter failure at home.

When I was accepted to Harvard, my family rejoiced—not because I would receive an excellent education, but because they would not need to find a man willing to marry and support me, something they had long considered impossible. To this day, when my brothers see my Dutch husband, they pat him gently on the back and say things like, "Are you all right? We know your life is very hard."

At Harvard, I took the terrible Chinese daughter thing a step further and decided I wanted to become a writer instead of a physicist. Although I was working up to four jobs to support myself, I found time for the dance lessons I had long desired. At the beginning, I was the worst student in every dance class. One dance teacher had to stifle a giggle in her sleeve after seeing my legs tangle themselves up. But I still loved dance and dreamed of finding grace—of becoming fierce, strong, in control of my body. And so I persevered.

After graduation, I moved back to New York City. Searching for a day job that would allow me to write at night, I spotted an ad in the paper that read, "Wanted: Professional Ballroom Dancer, Will Train." I was terrified to apply, but in the end, I did. During the grueling audition process, I could see that the other women were better trained, more coordinated, prettier, friendlier, and none of them were clumsy in the slightest. I stayed out of stubbornness and desire. I knew there was no chance they would give me the job. And yet, somehow, they did.

That was when my real training as a dancer began. My legs untangled themselves. I became aware of my center, my feet, my arms and head. I spent years teaching and performing in shows and competitions before I went to Columbia to get my MFA in fiction. I lied to my mother, who had never learned to speak English, and told her I was working as a computer programmer. I was busted years later, when

I had become a bestselling author and an interview about me and my dance past ran on the front page of the largest Chinese newspaper in the U.S.

But I'm still clumsy. The other professional dancers always teased me in a kind way about how my eyeliner was always crooked and my nails were a disgrace. I ask for no water when I appear on television because I'm likely to spill it on my interviewer. If someone throws a ball at me, I duck. I have crashed into more people and inanimate objects on my bicycle than I can count. No sane person would ever allow me to drive a car. And I am still problematic enough in the kitchen that when I asked my kids if they wanted me to make pancakes for them as a treat, they cried, "Oh no, not your pancakes!"

Imagine being in lockdown with a person like me as primary cook and caretaker. Thank goodness my husband does all of the cleaning. He took over the ironing as well after he saw the burns on my skin. He is, however, even more incompetent in the kitchen than I am. In these frightening times, when we are all separated from friends and family, I long for old-fashioned Chinese comfort food, which I have no idea how to make.

My mother passed away a number of years ago and I miss her terribly. As often happens, I realize that so much of what she tried to teach me was right: Don't cross against the light. Be kind to others. Good health is everything. Don't burn the rice.

I hear her voice in my head as my husband and kids stand around the trash can during our daily ritual of scraping burnt toast. I have hidden many a cooking misstep in the past but in lockdown, there are no more secrets. My thirteen-year-old son peered into the garbage, where I'd tossed some cookies that turned out, miraculously, both raw and charred, and said gently, "At least Papa won't get too fat this way."

And yet all is not lost. Something I learned from growing up in poverty is that happiness comes from within. We all have infinite resources—dreams, stories, hope—inside of us. We are rich if we have a roof over our heads, enough food to satisfy our hunger, love and kindness in our homes. My kids are learning to cook themselves and now keep an eagle eye on the oven if something yummy is baking in it. Although I haven't danced in years, the four of us prance around to dance apps every day to get some fun and exercise. It's goofy dancing, but it sparks the same joy as my old passion for dance. Perhaps even more, because now I can share it with the ones I love. We had very busy lives that would sometimes pull us all in different directions, but in this period of lockdown, we have learned to make time for each other again.

Finally, I find myself thinking about my clumsiness and my eternal search for grace. Grace, to me, is another word for compassion toward others and yourself. Perhaps grace is about not trying to fit a round peg into a square hole. Perhaps grace is finding your own unique strengths and developing those as best you can. Grace is doing what you love and loving what you do. So, in that sense, I suppose I can say that I have found grace during lockdown. And that maybe I'm not such a bad Chinese daughter after all.

JEAN KWOK is the award-winning, *New York Times* and international bestselling author of *Searching for Sylvie Lee, Girl in Translation,* and *Mambo in Chinatown.* Her work has been published in twenty countries and taught in universities, colleges, and high schools around the world.

THE FLOW ROOM

By Jessica Keener

Several nights ago, I woke up to a spinning room and nausea. I recovered quickly; I think it was a reaction to something I ate. But the brief incident sparked feelings of claustrophobia that are all too familiar to me. Living inside this weird pandemic bubble in 2020, a bubble that has no discernible membrane except the four walls of my house, is not unlike the three months in the winter of 1979, when I lived in a hospital isolation room, when my prince of a brother donated his bone marrow and saved my life.

Once again, as before, I am masking up, wearing gloves, sanitizing. I know this routine. I've lived it, but not with others. Not with the whole world.

Back then, I had just graduated college. My hospital room, which we called "the flow room" (short for laminar air flow room), was about eight by ten feet and designed to protect me from other people's germs. The sterilized room had a tiny window that looked onto a parking lot. I could see a patch of daylight and someone's car fender. There was nothing else to gaze upon, so I had to find ways to distract myself from the reality that I had only two options for getting out of that room one day: either alive or dead.

In the critical care unit, I got lethal doses of chemotherapy to destroy what remained of my malfunctioning bone marrow. In essence, my doctors killed me to save me. And it worked. I got through the initial tough days of nausea and flu-like symptoms. After that, my hair fell out, but I knew it would grow back. I started to feel well. I could get out, as long as I didn't get any infections. As long as my blood counts went up. As long as my immune system matured. But the timeline for all that happening was terribly unclear. I was among the first hundred in the world to get a bone marrow transplant for aplastic anemia, a rare blood disorder. My doctor said it could take two, three, five months. We would have to wait and see. This waiting became a mental game, similar to what we are all living with today because of COVID-19—waiting to get back to jobs, waiting to hug our elderly parents, waiting to return to the things that make us feel alive.

In my hospital room, thinking too far ahead could flood me with hard-to-breathe waves of depression, hopelessness, and boredom. So I tried not to think beyond the routines and tasks of the day: my morning bath, reading, listening to music, writing in my journal, breakfast, lunch, the daily visit with my primary nurse, who became my friend; the nightly visits and card games with my mother, and the TV shows I watched at night: *Columbo*, *Animal Kingdom*, and *The Golden Girls*. The next morning, I'd start over. How long would this go on? No one could give me a definitive answer. It felt endless.

I talked on the phone with friends and my boyfriend. Another week would pass and, despite my effort to stay positive, the heaviness in my head would return, making it hard to talk to people. During those harder days, I told the nurses not to let anyone visit me. Post a sign, I told them. *No Visitors Today*. I needed to be alone. In those darker moments, I felt like a bug in a glass jar, the lid screwed on. I was trapped, yet everyone could see me. I understood why animals paced in their cages. I began to pace. Every day, in circles. Listening to music. I paced.

Thankfully, the heaviness evaporated after a few days. Maybe I just needed to give myself a rest from positivity, which is an unnatural state to sustain all the time. I resumed seeing visitors and talking on the phone. But I continued to pace. It calmed me down.

I was not allowed to touch, let alone hug, anyone in the flow room. I lived behind a plastic barrier. Day after day, week after week, month after month—people came to visit me on the other side of a plastic curtain and then they went home and drove away in their cars while I remained inside my eight-by-ten, see-through box. It grew tiresome, as it is today, to live with the constant, unrelenting need to maintain social distance, wear masks, wash hands, wipe things down, sanitize — to wait to be released.

Perhaps the one significant difference I feel now is that I am not the pariah, the oddity I was back then. I am not the bug in a glass, the wild animal in a cage. No one had heard of my disease—or understood what a bone marrow transplant entailed. Today, everyone knows about COVID-19. I am just like everybody else. And, strange as this is to say, I am comforted by this. I am isolating, but this time, I am not alone.

JESSICA KEENER's latest novel, *Strangers in Budapest*, was an Indie Next pick, a Southern Independent bestseller, and an *Entertainment Weekly* "Best New Books" choice.

CONFINE

By Peter G. Quinn

We are asked to strand ourselves
make our house an island.

Protection Island out our window
now seems an elder.

How long will it be? What if it's longer
than the stalwart freezer can give?

How close to touch live skin
will we get again?

How often to venture out?
For what essential or forgotten thing?

Where will cash come from?
What bills can be paid?

Any checks in the mail today?
Pray tomorrow.

How long will
neighbor helping neighbor hold?

The world is focused
upon big cities at least

a coast away.
My little town shuttered and shuddering

braced for the maybe,
maybe the certainty of losing

store, job, neighbor, life.
The only certainty;

yesterday is gone.
Masks and soap

enough food and FedEx
the essentials – unless

they run out of things to deliver.
Patience is courage.

A red breasted house finch
flies in softer, lighter air,

its song a joyful hymn
calm, bright and free.

PETER G. QUINN is the author of the poetry collection *Painting Circles on Straight Highways*. He is cofounder of The Writers' Workshoppe and Imprint Books in Port Townsend, Washington.

THE HOUSE WITH THE MOSSY ROOF

By Abigail Carter

I walked my dog, Chloe, toward the house two doors down, the one with the mossy roof that we have passed nearly every day since moving to the neighborhood three years ago. I stopped at the driveway as Chloe sniffed a shrub, imagining myself climbing the crumbling steps, gripping the tilted iron railing, and knocking on the door. I imagined the yellowed sheets that served as drapes in the front window parting and a withered face appearing. I'd never seen the owner but knew he was an elderly man. How old, I had no idea.

"Yeah, he doesn't like to leave the house," his brother had told me last summer when I saw him doing yard work and stopped to talk. I'd always been curious about the person who lived there. "I do what I can to help," his brother said, "but I have my own house to keep up too, you know?" He said this as if asking my permission to get back into his red pickup and drive away.

Now, as I continued on my morning walk, I thought of what I might do to help this neighbor I'd never even seen. What would he think if I knocked on his door? Perhaps it would terrify him to have some stranger standing on his front porch, breathing potentially COVID-laden germs everywhere. Should I just leave a note?

I wondered if he was alone and frightened, watching (or listening?) to the news, not technically savvy enough to order groceries online. Was that ageism? He could be perfectly capable of initiating Zoom calls and caring for himself.

I did my best to help people where I could, and grocery store runs were part of my M.O. I imagined picking out a plump rotisserie chicken for my unknown neighbor, perhaps some apples, clementines, milk, bread, butter. Would he eat that stuff? What if I bought the wrong brands? Had his brother already stocked his cabinets full of food? Did he even cook? Maybe TV dinners? The menu of his life filled my head as I stooped with a long slender plastic bag that had held that morning's frightening headlines and now contained the morsel of poop laid by my small dog. Chloe pulled on her leash, yanking me farther away from the house with the mossy roof.

Would the man even want my help or resent the intrusion? Perhaps he'd be too frightened, fearful of contracting the virus that could kill him. Or perhaps he would welcome catching the virus.

I stopped walking. Had I really just had that thought? But the truth was, my own mortality followed me like a lost, hungry puppy. I was a single, widowed mother. Many times, since the first sniff of COVID-19 hit the airwaves, I thought I should pull out my will and review it, just in case. But I still hadn't done it.

During the nineteen years since my husband died, I had often thought of my own death as a way of finally being able to enjoy cocktails on the beach with Arron. What could be so bad? Of course, the thought was always knocked sideways the moment I thought of my leaving my daughter and son fully orphaned. I would feel like sobbing, imagining their grief over losing me too. They'd still been young then, but now I was a boomerang mom to adult children. If life ever got back to normal, my kids would scatter. Aloneness (not loneliness) was on my horizon.

My elderly neighbor's imagined desire for death, commingled with my own, followed me as I strode down the steep hill toward my local ravine, Dead Horse Canyon. Alone in the middle of the street, I laughed. Widow humor. Was this what happened when you were old and alone? You laugh in the middle of the street at anything death-related, the way teenagers laugh at anything sexual? I shook my head and continued, resolving to knock on the man's door on my way home. But later, as I walked past the house, my thoughts were filled with what I would make for dinner for me and my daughter. I still wasn't used to my daughter's gluten-free, plant-based diet, and became lost in thought about how to coax lentils, kale, and chickpeas into some kind of tasty concoction. This led me to think about French fries with gravy and cheese curds, full poutine style, the kind I used to get in Quebec visiting my grandparents. I didn't notice the house as I passed it.

The next day, I hesitated in front of the house again. *I should knock on the door*, I thought. *I really should knock.* I spotted a guy gardening in the next yard over. "Have you seen your neighbor?" I asked, expecting the worst.

"Sam? Oh sure. He's fine. He walks to the bus stop from time to time. His brother drops off groceries. It's sweet of you to ask."

"I'm glad," I said. I let out the breath I hadn't realized I was holding, as Chloe tugged on her leash.

ABIGAIL CARTER is the author of a memoir, *The Alchemy of Loss: A Young Widow's Transformation,* and a novel, *Remember the Moon.* Her essays have appeared in *SELF* magazine, *Reader's Digest, Seattle Magazine,* and *MORE* magazine.

145

DISASTER UNPREPAREDNESS

By Donna Miscolta

Long before this pandemic, long before my daughter tested positive for COVID-19, I was trained in the specter of disaster. I was born in 1953, within a decade of the start of the nuclear age.

In the late fifties, I did duck-and-cover drills with my classmates. We scrambled beneath our desks, cued by the screech of a siren. My face to the ground, arms wrapped around the back of my head, I believed that this is how our lives would be saved should bombs blast through the shelter of classroom furniture.

In the early sixties, I watched my mother stock a cupboard with canned goods, foods that we never knew came in a can, like brown bread. There was a tenseness to her stacking the cans three deep on the easily reachable lower shelf. When we asked what they were for, she demurred. But it was in the air—fear. And the words were on the news—Cuba, Castro, missiles. If the disaster came to pass, canned goods would save us.

In the eighties, bringing children into a world of nuclear arms escalation seemed either an act of faith or foolishness. When I was in my last trimester with my daughter Natalie, Chernobyl happened. Scientists projected the path of the nuclear cloud would cross over our Seattle home. Sheltering under a table with a stash of canned goods seemed a quaint and utterly useless safeguard against disintegrating atomic nuclei. In the end, the Chernobyl cloud, that invisible menace, drifted north of us.

Now another invisible menace has settled itself around the world, its U.S. epicenter in New York, where Natalie now lives. The makeshift hospital and truck morgues in Central Park are just blocks from her apartment, which is also situated between two major hospitals. The sirens transporting COVID-19 victims are a constant scream. The peril is always close and ever loud. The disaster I had been trained to expect was happening to my daughter.

Her work exposed her to the virus. She waited and wondered alone in her apartment. When would it strike her? How hard? Her head ached. She was tired. Were these symptoms? She rested in bed, took ibuprofen, downed tea for its herbal properties and Gatorade for its electrolytes. Her nights were sleepless with worry, her days plagued with fatigue. She lost her sense of smell. She knew that was a symptom, sure now that she was infected. A test confirmed it. Days later, her sense of smell returned, the fatigue abated, the occasional headache now more likely due to the strain of bearing the pandemic alone and the unthinkable what ifs had her symptoms been more severe.

Each evening at 6:55, her cat leaps to the sill in anticipation of the handclapping, banging, and cheers that pour from windows in support of the healthcare workers risking their lives to save others. Natalie throws open her window to shout. To breathe.

Donna Miscolta is the author of three books of fiction: *Living Color: Angie Rubio Stories*, *Hola and Goodbye: Una Familia in Stories*, and *When the de la Cruz Family Danced*. Her work has been published in *McSweeney's*, *Atticus Review*, *Necessary Fiction*, and other publications.

SUBURBAN NOCTURNE

By Sadia Hassan

Behind those trees, more trees which hide apartments
whose windows I surveil from my own.

A neighbor slick with sweat pulls dumbbells
past his bulging shoulders. Below him an American
flag slap boxes the air, petunias shiver over the railing.

How to protect one's heart from bruising under
what is not afraid to startle, what sees without sensing?

Four stories above the Boxwood and Cypress bushes,
the long shadow: a woman pacing under a flickering
porchlight.

The muffled cry of the Cameroonian mistress
on her miserable night walks? Is it French or Patois?

Did she leave him? Well, no. But who does not covet
a woman who will not leave? Instead, she turns
the shadowed staircase, flies up to her room.

From my own, I slip into a life of looped dreams
filled with nothing but this hunger.

In my dreams, I smell her off a lover. Taste the sea
in his ghost grip. All night the sky, our sheets, its Cimmerian crease—
stink of capsized boats. Behind the night, more night.

In the velvet stretch of dawn, I wake
non compos mentis, his mouth a blue spell

which stuns me. Behind those trees, a field
of the living, native plants flowering in Virginia's heat.
Summersweet. Switchgrass. Black-Eyed Susan.

SADIA HASSAN is an essayist, poet, and MFA candidate at the University of Mississippi. Her work has appeared in *Longreads,* *The Seventh Wave,* and the *Chattahoochee Review.* Her chapbook *Enumeration* appears in the New-Generation African Poets chapbook set *Saba.*

LAVENDER AND THE WASHING AWAY OF CIVILIZATIONAL ILLS

By Roberto Lovato

Take off your tragic airs, my dear friend, and fold them up and put them away in lavender. You'll never need them again.
—Lucy Maud Montgomery, *Anne's House of Dreams*

Pop spends most of the COVID-19 crisis sitting in his favorite leather recliner, head tilted on his left shoulder while he sleeps. During his waking hours—now becoming fewer and farther between—he waves at neighbors, watches action movies, or curses at strange dudes trying to park in his driveway. Next to Pop's recliner is a glass table with water, candies from his native El Salvador, and one of my most important tools for coping with COVID-19 and the civilizational crises it has exposed: lavender.

At almost ninety-eight years old, wheezing asthmatic Pop also suffers from dementia, a condition some studies say is improved by the "neuroprotective effects of inhaled lavender." The lack of control and perpetual enclosure brought on by COVID-19 make Pop's dementia worse, sometimes in exponentially bad and violent ways that require the power of the evergreen shrubs, hoary gray-green leaves, and purple flowers hidden in the lavender solution.

His dementia also makes him forget chunks of his life, like his childhood during a Great Depression in El Salvador that made *The Grapes of Wrath* look like a wine tasting. Pop's memory is also getting spotty about the bloody civil war in El Salvador in the 1980s, the decades of union struggles, and the life with and loss of his beloved wife, Maria Elena, my mom. Studies show that inhaling lavender oil helps children improve their ability to memorize a paragraph, and I secretly harbor the belief that it might hold out hope for Pop's memories too.

I've long used lavender in daily rituals—shaving, applying facial cream, drinking lavender tea at La Boheme, my favorite coffee shop—to aid my own memory. Lavender reminds me who I was before COVID-19, who I am, and who I aspire to be. Even before all of our lives changed in March, I used it to remind me of and carry me through the many civilizational calamities I've witnessed—and overcome—as a journalist and activist.

When I visited El Salvador in the late eighties and early nineties, during the civil war that left eighty thousand dead, most of them murdered by the U.S.-backed government, I brought lavender cream from a bougie shop in San Francisco. The cream soothed my skin and calmed my nerves after seeing the effects of bombings and strafing on innocent civilians, including children. After I was pursued by death squads in El Salvador, lavender bubble baths were there for me. This hygienic practice dates back to the Romans, who named the divine plant *Lavandula*, Latin for "to wash." The irony of using the bathing ritual of the ancient imperium to wash away the evils of the contemporary empire never escaped me.

More recently, lavender soap, lavender jade Buddhist prayer beads, and lavender eye pillows were part of the soothing rituals I used after my goddaughter and I were chased by *maras*, gun-wielding Salvadoran gang members, while we were saying goodbye to my deceased mother in the small cemetery of her hometown, San Vicente.

Lavender has long been there for humanity, even when our civilizations fall tragically short of our ideals. As the Roman empire began to decline, due in part to the advent of Christianity, the authors of what would become the New Testament started hailing the powers of spikenard (from the Greek name for lavender, *nardus*), the powerful plant with which Mary "anointed the feet of Jesus, and wiped his feet with her hair; and the house was filled with the odor of the ointment." Since then, generations of Christians have believed lavender—dubbed the "broom of the brain" by ancient East Indians because it supposedly swept away foul humors—has the power to ward off evil.

Salvadorans have long known about the "decline of American civilization" that some are only now discovering thanks to COVID-19. I have thought a lot about this during the eight-mile hikes that are my primary escape from the confines imposed on us by the epidemic. Along the way, I indulge in my other source of great escape: hiking on urban trails lined with lavender, the same lavender I use in the hopes it helps with Pop's past—and my future.

It has been over sixty days since the quarantine began. My most recent hikes still find me picking lavender, but I'm now focusing on a post-COVID-19 future that includes a new friend, R. I met R., a fellow journalist, several months before the pandemic hit the U.S., when she interviewed me for an online magazine. I liked her thoughtful line of questioning, but she doesn't live in San Francisco, and our friendship blossomed during the spring of COVID-19. As a result, we have never met in person. Our connection has grown almost entirely through the technology of a more romantic era: the phone.

We debated the possibility of "taking things to the next level" with Zoom, but we worried about introducing visual stimuli into the virtuous connection of our voices. Finally, after some back and forth, we scheduled a Zoom call for a Saturday night in April.

I dealt with my nervousness in my usual way: taking a hike and picking lavender. I carpeted the corner of the kitchen table that's now my work station with calming purple buds, turned on the Zoom link R. had sent, and picked up a sprig of fresh lavender from the table, calmed by its suzzy purple and green goodness. The Zoom screen opened, and I stood breathless, as if inhaling a bong hit, before a handsome, black-haired woman with a smart, kind look in her eyes. I smiled awkwardly. So did she.

After our initial uncertainty, we eased into the breezy talk we'd enjoyed for several weeks. The visual factor expanded and enhanced the connection of our voices.

"You like lavender?" she asked me, noting the sprig.

"Yes. I love it."

Our faces lit up, because within R.'s reach was the creamy delight of lavender lotion and a lavender heat/cold pouch her sister-in-law had given her. We were both smelling lavender.

We've continued talking. Our voices remain our primary source of connection, with Zoom reserved for special Saturday nights. But we've also made plans to see each other the old-fashioned, pre-COVID-19 way. In anticipation of that first physical encounter, I take a hike and pick the lavender I will have with me when we meet.

Roberto Lovato is a journalist and author of *Unforgetting: A Memoir of Family, Migration, Gangs, and Revolution in the Americas.*

SONG AT THE END OF THE MIND

By Susan Rich

I think of you as a radio frequency—
(sometimes hard to find)

as I touch this illuminated dial.
But tonight you arrive

murmuring into my ear in half-sleep;

you offer a suitcase of small pleasures
and laughter that somersaults across the country.

In this time of shelter in place,
we are fevered wanderers

with nothing but an open screen;

handheld devices offering luminous ellipses.
We heal the earthquaked bones

of our pasts decorating rough mouths
with new vocabularies—

no longer deferred.

As the world quiets,
I'm awake to our longings.

All that is left: to congregate
close along the shoreline

unbandaged and unadorned;

to listen to the smooth rhythm and cues
of Quarantine Radio.

This one goes out to you.

SUSAN RICH is the author of four collections of poetry and winner
of the PEN USA Award and Peace Corps Writers Award. She has two
books forthcoming, *Gallery of Postcards and Maps: New and Selected
Poems* (Salmon Press) and *Blue Atlas* (Red Hen Press).

PART FOUR: CONNECT

Claudia Castro Luna, the Poet Laureate of Washington State, wrote this poem the day after George Floyd was murdered. She wrote it thinking of COVID-19, thinking of the need for immigration reform, thinking of the upcoming 100th anniversary of women's suffrage. "The tree at the end alludes to our country's horrific history of lynching," Castro Luna says. "Let us not forget because trees don't."

HER WAY

- FOR PRAMILA JAYAPAL -

By Claudia Castro Luna

It matters how we walk the world
to see with heart matters
to acknowledge grief
to see in others the same sparkle
so familiar in our own mother's eye
to learn the old names
to say them with dignity, that is important
courage is not a crown
more like chattering of teeth
the knot in the stomach
at choosing the long hard way
owning what is not known
that, takes courage
and knowing that hunger
can be for bread as for justice
having a glimpse of home is part of it
not homes had, but the ones to build
where there will be room

for everyone at the table
and for those who only want
a cool glass of lemonade
there will be a porch
on the sunny side of the street
under the knowing eye
of a wise, nearby tree

CLAUDIA CASTRO LUNA is the Washington State Poet Laureate
(2018 - 2021), Seattle's first Civic Poet (2015-2017), an Academy of
American Poets Laureate Fellow, and author of *This City; One River, A
Thousand Voices;* and Pushcart-nominated *Killing Marias.*

STATE OF THE ART, STATE OF THE UNION

By Devi S. Laskar

You are red.

Red-cheeked, raging at the TV, mourning for all those who have died needlessly.

You are also the red sirens of the ambulances that frequent your California streets in this age of infection and disease.

You are a want, the wanting to reach a distant shore, to swim in a red sea, so named before it inevitably dies.

You are a want, a return to some semblance of normalcy.

You want to visit your family living on the other side of the country in a state where the lawmakers do not believe in science.

You are a decades-old memory: the red of India, your red-gold bridal sari glistening in the sun.

You are wanted, unwanted.

In this election season, in this dim understanding of virus without vaccine and the semantics between sheltering in place and staying at home, you offer what you can.

Sometimes you write poems. Poetry in wartime is a luxury. Poetry in wartime is a necessity.

Sometimes you take photographs. You try to document what's still visible.

Sometimes you still dream.

Sometimes you say you are a writer, sometimes you say you are a poet, sometimes you say you have not the faintest clue what you are today.

You try to call your family and warn them. You tell them to listen to your governor, since their governor is more concerned about money.

Another day with electronic messages scrolling across your screen in red and black, warning you not to go out unless necessary; another tally mark of self-quarantine.

Another short walk with camera in hand: mask and sunglasses on face, hoping to see through the lens darkly what you can point at, shoot.

You have not observed a cardinal in many days but have noticed the red ants taking up residence in the garage. In the evenings, the red cedars appear alight under the setting sun.

There is red rust along the mouth of the bathtub drain, a hawk spiraling toward a red siskin perched on a branch, a red spider glistening in the light of a star, uncorked cabernet going to vinegar, and a doctor on cable news speaking of red blood cell counts as you polish the pair of new pennies in your pocket.

You still want to write, you still want to finish the story you've been toiling over for years.

Yet you are distracted by numbers you see on TV: the death tolls, the number of those infected, the shortages of personal protective equipment and hospital beds and breathing apparatuses, the shortages of food in many corners of the American landscape, the lines of cars that stretch toward infinity outside food banks.

You used to be a reporter. You remain grateful other reporters are still asking tough questions, still seeking the truth. Especially now. You want to know but sometimes you can't bear it.

The televised press conference *du jour* offers solutions for other diseases, but not the one coursing through the American body. This illness that has killed more Americans in three months than the sum of American lives lost during the wars in Korea and Vietnam combined. There are no national plans for widespread testing, no national plans to contact trace those who have become infected and/or unwittingly carry it.

In this election season, the candidates and lawmakers make so many beautiful, impossible promises. History books say politicians from America's bloody beginnings bargained with turquoise and diseased blankets. Now, they bargain with surgical masks and ventilators, and paper currency—they tell your neighbors in neighboring states to go back to work because your lives are worthless if there is no American marketplace.

As a poet you still wonder how to rhyme words like dangerous and marathon, month, opus, orange, pint, purple, silver, wolf. Then you open a book and find a solution: taking a slant on the situation, a twist of the tongue. Suddenly orange can hang with boring, door-hinge, forage, lozenge, and porridge. You are almost giddy for a moment; you can almost forget about the diseased American body when you are lost in words.

Seventy days of sitting still instead of preparation as part of the national response. Seventy days that included golfing and campaign rallies and wishing aloud for miracles.

The people in charge fancy themselves as knowledgeable, trustworthy.

Yet they want to drown the American body in disinfectant and ultraviolet light, and they want to drown out the voices of the scientists begging them to stop their conjecture.

What appears on the magic landscape of the computer: a recipe for bitter orange soup, panorama shots of fruit groves and dairy farms as the voiceover talks about food shortages, an ocean shoreline besieged by tourists in defiance of a governor's order to stay indoors.

What is disappearing: forests, recycling and environmentalism, the regulations for organic food, nonviolence, the green flash of atmospheric refraction at dusk, your optimism, vehicle emission standards, toilet paper, clean water standards, birds, rhinos, green rivers, and seas free of trash.

When you live in the midst of a pandemic, every waking hour is plagued with thoughts of worst-case scenarios, what ifs and contingency plans.

What if you get sick and die?
What if your children or your ailing parents or your loved ones are alone?

All of your opinions about the rest of the world and the other problems begin to mute themselves in your head. You want to keep arguing for those things you were passionate about fifty days ago, but you cannot remember what day of the week it is, you cannot remember the month. What were your thoughts on forever wars, civil rights, women's rights, global warming, plant and animal extinction, cruelty to children and to wild and domesticated animals?

On the news, you watch people waving confederate flags, in defiance of their states' stay-at-home orders. Angry people who believe the virus serves as a political ploy. They wave their flags and chant their right to bear arms but cannot grasp the idea that you cannot shoot your way out of a situation involving an invisible disease.

Some people work hard to make life more equitable.
Others love to watch it all burn to the ground.

While the doctors and nurses and some state lawmakers beg the population to stay indoors, others deny droughts, tornados, famine, ethnic cleansing, school shootings, systemic racism, and diseases like

COVID-19. They deny the periodic table and Darwin's theory of evolution.

You rage at the TV. Your voice grows as hoarse as when your allergies bloom in response to lilies and lavender.

You wait in line at the post office, masked: You see bodies of privilege scoff at the signs that direct all those who enter to cover their noses and mouths. They refuse to listen, demand service.

You wait in line at the grocery store, masked: You see the security guard turn away an older man who will not wear a mask.

You wonder if it will be safe to fly in what remains of this calendar year.
You wonder if you'll ever see your mother or father in person again.

You see your family and friends via cell phone, via computer. Your hair is grayer. There are circles under everyone's eyes, there are worry lines accenting the corners of mouths.

In Georgia a man is shot and killed for jogging while being black. Ten years since the state police in Georgia raided you and yours. Ten years since baseless accusations were first hurled at your husband by his former employer. Six long years of fighting back. Four years since a state judge dismissed all of the unfounded charges, and your family was finally free.

Yet your PTSD lingers like a bad cold.

You are triggered by anything, and everything, and nothing.

Devi S. Laskar's debut novel, *The Atlas of Reds and Blues* (Counterpoint Press, 2019) is winner of the Asian/Pacific American Award for Literature and the Crook's Corner Book Prize. A former newspaper reporter, she is now a poet, photographer, and novelist. She lives in California.

BEHIND YOUR FACE

By Lise Haines

My favorite was the horse mask. I was eight and it was Halloween. I had a flannel horse suit that tied at the back of my neck, a pillowcase for candy, and I knew the people in all the homes in my neighborhood. My family was coming unglued, soon to pack up and move away. But on that night, through the big eyeholes of a wild horse, I saw only abundance. Maybe I'll never care for another mask as much.

I once loved a man who had a collection of masks. Wood and paper, tin and clay. I imagined traveling around the world with him to learn his expressions. But we stayed home and I learned a couple of them scared me, even when I hid them in a box above the closet. After our love disappeared, I began to wear an invisible mask. It looks like my face when I put it on. I can smile behind it and no one can see what I'm doing.

In Tokyo last summer with my sister and her husband, masks were black and plentiful. Through Shinagawa station, people moved in all directions at once but never collided. Now most of us wear masks and move in wider orbits. We cut up T-shirts and pajamas, stitch them into soft protection, write colorful things across our faces. As if there's something to say before we go.

I wonder if we will ever see expressions again, those signs of love and forgiveness.

Before quarantines, grocery deliveries, and body counts, I once saw a couple in a Starbucks. His entire face was visible but only her eyes. She was a mask wearer. He leaned close and whispered. He kissed her without touching her. That was love. Something that penetrated her mask.

LISE HAINES's latest novel is *When We Disappear* (2018). Her work also appears in *AGNI*, *Ploughshares*, and other journals. She is senior writer in residence at Emerson College.

DEAR O

By Ching-In Chen

I was born, they said, a boy
into a heritage of paper

If a fire is placed in a crumbling wall
it leads me to you, separated from the screen

I am not here often

The one who arrived, I lost him in the sea

I was born
so much missing your eyesight
blooming without birds

My body unfolds
and the sound it sings in line

I lost you in the sea.
An ideal neighbor a stone buried below my mother's whitegrain building

A blue vat dye, burning stones to throw

All my unborn reckless as a lamp
strung as a light
broke a path

There was a boy who was not me
because I was a bird singing double-
hearted in the floating line by the sea

soft-throated to face down
the audience

CHING-IN CHEN is the author of *The Heart's Traffic, recombinant* (winner of the 2018 Lambda Literary Award for Transgender Poetry), *how to make black paper sing,* and *Kundiman for Kin: Information Retrieval for Monsters.* Chen is also the co-editor of *The Revolution Starts at Home: Confronting Intimate Violence Within Activist Communities* and *Here Is a Pen: an Anthology of West Coast Kundiman Poets*

ECSTATIC STATES

By Lidia Yuknavitch

An Alone

What I mean is this: when I am alone I experience the electrical charge of full embodiment and full being in a way that I cannot when I am in the world with people. Rapture lives here, the bite cutting clean through the tether to togetherness. Fit me inside making art. Sew me back inside the waters of the imaginal.

You have to lure me out with the meat of you every time. You have to trick me into coming clean.

I understand how that sounds, I understand that the whole point to living a life as a human mammal is connection with other humans. Everyone knows that, right? I'm reminded of it every nanosecond of my life from everyone (or nearly everyone) I encounter. I'm directly and indirectly shamed for my devotion and attraction to aloneness. Even from people who claim to "know" me and deeply "love" me. I mean, if you truly want to be alone more often than you want to connect with others, there must be something a little bit wrong with you. Right? You must have some wound or you have not fully integrated the parts of yourself or you have not finished learning the value of human interconnection. You're stunted. Underdeveloped. Possibly worse. So I'm told.

What if my strongest connections happen with water, rocks, trees, dirt, colors, sounds, ideas?

Sometimes animals.

What if I feel closest to the people we send away, the people on some edge, the people who prefer the room of alone, farthest from the verve and thrust of people pushing human connection and the flush and scurry of social synergy?

Aloneness looks different on me. I'm in love with aloneness. I desire aloneness. I crave it. There is an erotics inside the alone. I leave the social contract every day, my letting-go hand suspended in the air, the lost treasure of our meeting.

Lost Treasure

In 1901 an object was retrieved from the bottom of the sea amid a wreck off the coast of the Greek island Antikythera. The object was dated around 70-60 BC. The Antikythera mechanism, as it came to be known, was an ancient Greek machine used to predict astronomical positions and the motion of the sun and moon. It is the most sophisticated mechanism known from the ancient world; we know of nothing as complex from the next thousand years. The device was found as one lump down in the depth of blue, later separated into three main fragments which are now divided into eighty-two separate fragments. Four of these fragments contain gears. The largest gear is approximately 5.5 inches in diameter and originally had 223 teeth.

Lost Tooth

In 1976, a thirteen-year-old girl sits on a deep blue shag rug in her family living room. *The Undersea World of Jacques Cousteau* animates the television. The smell of cigarette smoke curls its way around her from her father's architecture study. The girl is grateful he has work tonight so that he is not in the living room in the black leather recliner watching *Jacques Cousteau* with her, or she would feel the heavy, almost not able to breathe feeling of her father weighing down her chest, her lungs, her heart, her hips. Instead, just his smoke. The girl is quietly grateful she is nothing about that grotesque word *family* in this moment. The girl is being her aloneness, the most beautiful state of being she has ever known. Because of its brevity and purity. Something lost and forgotten about—maybe something lost and forgotten at the bottom of the ocean. That silence. Seaweed swaying in the deep undulating current. She runs her hands across the deep blue shag carpet pretending it is the ocean. She closes her eyes. The voice of Jacques Cousteau makes her hips ache. That's when her hand hits something hard, like a tiny piece of gravel, embedded in the carpet. She opens her eyes. She digs for it. She holds the object up to her face. It's a tooth. A tiny tooth. A child tooth. She holds the tooth between her thumb and forefinger and studies the tiny tooth in front of her face. Beyond the tooth she sees Jacques Cousteau talking on the television, his red knit hat. She smells cigarette smoke. She puts the tooth into her mouth. She wonders how many teeth live at the bottom of the ocean, how many girls, is anyone diving for them? She swallows.

Alone

The sea swallows everything of us. But sunken treasures have a way of rearranging the story. A ship at the bottom of the sea folds gently over into sand and barnacle and sea creature ecosystems, losing its former worth and moorings, for a ship is built and meant to float. Its sinking is a kind of failure of humanity, but not for ocean beings. The ship changes forms when it goes from sailing the surface to wrecked at the bottom. The wreck changes forms after the dead people disintegrate and the cargo settles to sand. The fish find homes and hiding places. Radars take years to detect the great masses driven off course. Whole histories and meanings drop from existence only to be rediscovered and attached to stories we make up because we need them to mean something besides nothing. When someone finds the sunken thing, new value emerges. We need human history to mean something besides nothing. We need the things we do with our hands to mean something and not nothing. We need the sunken treasure to mean something of human value was once lost and yet found again, something of ourselves was salvaged and brought back in pieces to the surface, something we thought dead and gone yet holds life. Delicate truths, delicate artifacts.

Fish don't need anything of people.

The Solitude of Objects

ar·ti·fact

/ˈärdəfakt/

noun

1. an object made by a human being, typically an item of cultural or historical interest. "gold and silver artifacts"

2. something observed in a scientific investigation or experiment that is not naturally present but occurs as a result of the preparative or investigative procedure. "Widespread tissue infection may be a technical artifact."

Origin: early nineteenth century: from Latin *arte* "by or using art" + *factum* "something made" (neuter past participle of *facere* "make").

The Subjectivity of Objects

When the girl was five, she used to fill small boxes with sticks and moss and rocks to make a pretend family. The sticks were their bodies and the rocks were their hearts and the moss was their hair. She would sing to the pretend family she would tell the pretend family bedtime stories she would rock the pretend family, boxes cupped in her hands, before putting on the lids at night. The families had no heads, no brains or mouths or teeth. They had no arms or legs or hands. Just stick bodies and rock hearts and moss hair. She kept three boxes of families made from sticks and rocks and moss underneath her pillow. If she shook one of the boxes the rattling sound comforted her. Like a baby's rattle. One day her father found the boxes underneath her pillow. The girl began to cry. This is crybaby shit. Only babies put boxes of crap under their pillows. Cut out this baby shit.

The girl wailed inside her alone.

That night she snuck out of the house, dug through the trash outside, found the boxes of her created artifacts, and buried them in the backyard underneath a tree. Before she closed the boxes to bury them, she spit in them so that her DNA would bind and hold the little hidden family forever.

Whale story

In 2018, the orca named J35 finally let go of her dead calf in the waters off the Pacific Northwest coast. She had pushed the dead calf with her head for nearly seventeen days and one thousand miles. It was the longest recorded example of an orca mourning. The scientists studying her pod, the J Pod of Southern Resident Killer Whales, nick-named her Tahlequah. The scientists said she "appears to be in good physical condition" even after her "tour of grief."

J35 bonded with her calf after birth for about thirty minutes before it died. Some scientists believe that's why the mother would not break with the neonate.

Her baby whale head and mouth surfaced every so often as mother pushed daughter mile after mile, as if the space between living and dead opened up in the mother waters even though everyone everywhere thought the story had ended.

Lost and Found

The most ecstatic moment of my life happened in such a quiet moment that sometimes, at my age, I have trouble remembering it. This troubles me. If I can't locate the memory, if it drifts fully away to sea, sinks to the bottom, does that mean my joy is irretrievable, gone to the alone?

Remember to go down again. Dive into the wreck. Bite the tether. Swim home. Bring back something useful for others so they need not drown. It is enough.

LIDIA YUKNAVITCH is the author of the memoir *The Chronology of Water* and the novels *The Small Backs of Children, Dora: A Headcase,* and *The Book of Joan.*

PANDEMIC DATE NIGHT

By Sommer Browning and David Shields

D: Maybe we should watch EYES WIDE SHUT?

S: I don't remember it very well, but nobody is funnier than Tom Cruise.

D: All queued up?

S: I need a few minutes—like 3?

D: If you're late again, I'm going to slap yr gorgeous ass . . .

S: . . . til it knows who its master is? I'll never be on time, then!

D: LOL.

S: Okay, I'm ready.

D: Action!

S: I forgot TC was a doctor.

D: He's standing on a box and she's still a foot taller than he is.

S: She must have a UTI.

D: Kidman? Pourquoi?

S: She has to pee so much . . . I can't type what I want to say to you fast enough. I need to be next to youuuuuu.

D: "The Latin poet Ovid had a very good time"—WTF? He's from Brazil?

S: Hahaha.

D: This guy graduated summa cum laude from the Porn School of Acting.

S: You don't believe that Hungarian accent?

D: Unfortunately, he looks exactly like my urologist.

S: HOTT.

D: Uh oh a dead naked lady.

S: A dead naked MANDY.

D: Sidney Pollack actually just said, "This stays between us."

S: Kind of a terrible cut to office, or just super weird?

D: The name of the character who is hitting on Kidman is "Sky du Mont." The movie is bad line by line and shot by shot?

S: I think it's bad on purpose.

D: We need to zoom in on the books on the dresser. What are they?

S: INTRODUCTION TO SCIENTOLOGY, Vols 1-4.

D: I like this moment coming up: she would give up everything for the naval officer. She gave it all up for Keith Urban?

S: LOL. She'll even give up her child? Everyone wants to destroy themselves?

D: Phew. Phone call rescues us from the bad acting.

S: I want you to answer the phone while we're naked in bed and say, "Yes, this is Dr. Shields." I would cum all over you.

D: Another Hungarian acting audition now, by someone from Scarsdale.

S: These people are so fucking repressed. TC literally just said, "Michigan is a beautiful state." Or a wonderful state. Or something.

D: Film is loosely based, I think, on an Arthur Schnitzler novella, so it's as if Kubrick hasn't figured out how to translate 1920s Vienna into

1999 NYC.

S: It makes zero sense.

D: Film should be retitled CONTINUITY ERRORS.

S: This street scene is hilarious. What kind of NYC is this?!

D: TC can't even slap his hands together correctly.

S: How much does it cost to do a prostitute's dishes?

D: Is she a flight attendant for Pan Am, ca. 1977?

S: It really is a weird movie. But I get what it's going for, I think.

D: Tell me—

S: Some kind of investigation of desire under the hegemony of monogamy and domesticity? Everything is entirely unbelievable—on purpose, it seems. That's the part I can't fit in.

D: I just think it's a bad movie. He made it on a sound stage in London and hadn't visited real life in 20 years.

S: Right after he filmed the moon landing?

D: LOL. This is the most boring movie I've ever watched. Impossible to justify its tedium, from my POV. It's so fun to text w you, tho.

S: It is pretty bad.

D: I love your reading of it. . . . I like how you said your friend Leon is an asshole at times, but you love him. I sometimes don't get there w people.

S: My friend Marc is also an asshole. I shouldn't get there w people. But I keep them at a distance so they don't hurt my feelings.

D: It's the 30,000-foot view. Serbian, in a way? But sometimes people are just assholes. I'm probably too good at saying, "You're bad for me—you're out of my life." I love you so fucking much.

S: My favorite part of this movie is when TC holds down the napkin for the piano player so he can write the password.

D: It's the least sexy movie in word cinema.

S: "Word cinema" is amazing! I want to be w you so bad.

D: Can we never part? . . . The next hour is a slog. I wonder if we just scrub fwd post-saturnalia.

S: We can stop watching, if you want. If we went to a sex thing like this, we would have a good time.

D: I love how you said we have somewhat mysteriously decided to pay close attn to each other. Let's never stop.

S: Only TC can't get laid at an orgy.

D: I was once at Studio 54 where it was like this. My one experience of such.

S: Really—people fucking out in the open?

D: Pretty much. Everyone on coke. AIDS hadn't hit yet.

S: Sounds bananas.

D: Sex clubs v diff?

S: People aren't high.

D: How do ppl deal w STD issues?

S: At the sex club, you can do as little or as much as you want, so you can avoid intercourse if you want.

D: I must admit I would want to avoid getting an STD via oral sex at sex club—anything that would inhibit our lovemaking. Is that a very boring thing to acknowledge?

S: No, it's not.

D: If we make it through this movie together, our bond is unbreakable.

S: Seriously. This is v hard. . . . Going to sex clubs is not that important to me—just so you know.

D: I'm very interested and would at least like to check it out . . . This hotel clerk is the most natural actor in the film, by far.

S: I love him!

D: He's having fun. No one else is. He's alive. Everyone else is a corpse.

S: I will do anything w you.

D: What a beautiful thing to say. Thank you. I will try to do same for you. . . . TC can't even drive like a normal human being.

S: Oh no—more bad Sibelius.

D: I'm learning so much in therapy. Hugely centered around, Fuck, just say what you're feeling and thinking. Own who you are. Be authentic to yourself and the world. Forget about "should." Go with instinct. Duh.

S: It's scary: showing who you are and what you want IRL. First, it's hard to even know what you want.

D: You're good at it: "I don't want us to work on the film anymore." That was so good: take me or leave me; I love myself; you may love me, if you wish. So easy! We will get great at it together. I am so excited to do that w each other.

S: So easy. Haha.

D: The music!

S: It's insane!

D: VERONA in background in neon for 2 mins in case you didn't know what movie was about yet.

S: I do miss New York; this movie can do that at least . . . I miss yr body so much.

D: I know how very lucky I am to have met you. I will never let you go.

S: Reading that is incredible. I love you. . . . Oh no—John Prine.

D: He'd been ill for weeks. There are songs of his I love to death.

S: I know only the song you sent me.

D: Will send a few faves. My goal in life is to make a movie good enough to run "It's a Big Old Goofy World" under the end credits.

S: Ughhhhhhh I can't wait until you get here. And I can pinch you. And we can listen to music. And drink coffee. That's all I want.

D: What will we do first? (Rhetorical question?)

S: Fuckshowercrykiss.

D: Cuz we do everything backwards. We fell in love in Amsterdam, then met in LA. We will die on Montauk and be born many moons later in Kuala Lumpur.

S: We will crawl back into the sea together.

SOMMER BROWNING is a poet and writer living in Denver. Her books include *Backup Singers, Either Way I'm Celebrating, Poet-Librarians in the Library of Babel, You're on My Period*, and several others.

DAVID SHIELDS has written way too many books, one of which—*Reality Hunger*—*LitHub* recently named one of the one hundred most important books of the last decade, which now, of course, seems like last century. His work has been translated into two dozen languages.

SEDUCTION, AFTER FRUIT & MERCY

By Serena Chopra

Love, is there enough that the body can't do
that it won't do
for herself—

the way a pomegranate gives seed by seed
so little, a great pleasure.

Excess is a shadow suffered—

the cat finds me indulgent
in her empty hours with windows
my opaque patterns of coffee, dishes, dressing
hunger detached as the day swelling
from its ligament of pointed hours

healing is
without you, I can't
but do
anyway I need
but need
wantless.

What the body can't, won't—
       this fantasy of knife or rind.

In these hours of rigid organ
a chill fractures

a totem breaks in my jaw
some effort of life
rests over the cat—her meals, her beds,
her redundant demands
to mine.

Isn't there enough pain, Love,
in the world for you
not to be paining too?

Isn't there enough that the body can do—

Won't stop
healing.

even torn flesh muted even
I don't scar torn
quotidian swell flushing with battery
blushing each bruise
like condensation, lifted
fresh.
                    What tears me is father
                    land man
                    hood citizen
                    ship war
                    like tender
                    foot mother
                    tongues scar
                    tissues in the weather
        of two inaccurate suicides, wrists
steady as a painting—

to breathe these oxygens
to mend in cells

like history, Love
like forests, Love
like children, Love
like wantless love—

SERENA CHOPRA is an assistant professor of creative writing
at Seattle University, a writer, dancer, filmmaker, and visual and
performance artist. She has two books, *This Human* and *Ic*, as well as
two films, *Dogana/Chapti* (Official Selection at Frameline43, Oregon
Documentary Film Festival and Seattle Queer Film Festival) and
Mother Ghosting.

ZOOMING THE SUBTLE BODY

By Dawn Raffel

Imagine you are walking along a beach in the late afternoon at the end of summer. You have this stretch of sand all to yourself. A few gulls are circling, calling to one another. The heat of the day has lifted and there's a breeze coming off the ocean. You can feel that breeze on your skin and in your hair. The sand is warm and soft under your bare feet.

Up ahead you see a large conch shell. You admire its spiraling shape, and you know that this shell was once a home. You can't see all the way into the innermost chamber, but you see that the inside is lined with a luminous pearlescent pink. You hold the shell to your ear, and you hear a sound that sounds like the ocean, and you are reminded of nature's symmetries—and the way the infinite reposes in the infinitesimal.

You take the shell away from your ear and hold it for a moment longer in your hand, feeling its weight and its texture. Then you return it to the sand where you found it. You continue to walk, close to the water's edge . . .

Now imagine you are lying flat on your back, in a darkened room, in the middle of a pandemic. You haven't seen much of anything outside your increasingly claustrophobic walls for the past . . . who knows how long. The days, weeks, and months have lost their contours. Is it March or May? Your hair has grown long, your patience short. Your heart is sore. *The beach, the breeze, the shell, the sand* . . . they are all conjured: via speaker, via code, via modem or WiFi, via the wiring of the brain and the biology of the body, via layers of the conscious and subconscious mind, via memory, via emotion, via an ancient wisdom tradition.

This is yoga *nidra*, via Zoom.

———

Say *yoga* and most people envision down-dogs and headstands, but physical movement is only one component of yoga, which, despite all attempts to commercialize it, remains rooted in Vedic philosophy. If thousands of plank poses give you flat abs, then good for you. But the purpose of yoga (to write it on the head of a pixel) is to overcome the obstacle of the mind so that we can experience our true nature. In other words, it's an inside job.

Yoga *nidra*, which I teach, is a meditative practice done entirely in Savasana[2]—the flat-on-back pose usually associated with the end of a movement class, a rest after breaking a sweat. Yoga *nidra* is a cousin of sorts to this short, sweet, familiar Savasana: For twenty minutes or half an hour (longer, if you're going deep), the body remains still; only the consciousness moves, following a script with specific steps.

By the time I lead my class to the beach, we've already scanned the mind space, planted the seeds of a change we'd like to make or an action we'd like to take, "rotated" the consciousness in a guided tour of the body, witnessed the breath and counted it backward, and experienced dualities such as heaviness and lightness. All of this is in service of entering the richly fertile state between wakefulness and sleep.[3]

The beach scene, which continues for a few more minutes, is an example of dharana (concentration), intended to focus and further

2 Most people don't love contemplating that Savasana in English is "corpse pose."
3 In scientific terms, you might call it an alpha wave state.

calm the mind. It's written by the individual teacher—in this case, me. In part because I'm a writer, I tend to change it up for each session (seashell, forest, flower . . . it varies, and it doesn't). The remainder of the script will be fairly uniform in any class, anywhere, continuing with a series of rapid visualizations and a letting go of thought.

Yoga *nidra* is remarkably effective in easing stress-related fatigue and insomnia—two of the few things of which there have been no shortage in recent months. It also helps practitioners tap into deeper layers of consciousness and creativity, which is why I often teach it to writers (otherwise known as overthinkers). Pre-COVID-19, I had come to love the energy of the shared physical space, the subtlety of interactions, the connectedness of "sleeping together."

To Zoom a yoga *nidra* class, with each of us disembodied, felt attenuated, strange. And then it didn't. The coding that makes technology possible—like pretty much everything in our lived experience, from systems of thought and belief, to systems of physical roots, to electric circuits, to fragile ecosystems on land and at sea, to our conscious and unconscious selves, to replicable pathogens—is interconnected.

––––––––

There is no known cure for the virus that forced us indoors and apart, scorching hundreds of thousands of people with loss and grief. I'm grateful that, as of this writing, I have my health and so does my family. But no one has been immune to the sadness all around us.

I once read that the cure for sadness is to learn something new.[4] And so, mid-pandemic, I registered for an intensive training (on

4 "The best thing for being sad . . . is to learn something new" is a quote from *The Once and Future King*, a novel by T.H. White that is based on the legends of King Arthur. As with many inspirational quotes, it has gained a kind of viral currency in popular culture.

Zoom, of course) in *prana vidya*. This rarely-taught system of yoga meditation focuses on the life force carried with the breath, also called "the subtle body." Each day, I listened to my teacher (who was thousands of miles away), concentrated on seeing the unseeable within and without my body, and communed with students in time zones all over the world.

One definition of yoga is "union." Yoga enfolds duality and can elide the boundaries of the most stubbornly paradoxical human concepts. Zooming the subtle body? Why not?

———

People who teach yoga do it because it brings them joy. For all that I thrive on taking classes in movement, prana meditation, and yoga *nidra*, nothing gives me the high I get while teaching it. Of course I enjoy it when students tell me they finally got a decent night's sleep or untangled a knot, but I can't take credit for that. What I pass along is no more mine than the water in the ocean. The deepest peace I experience is in the moments when I feel this wisdom tradition flowing through me, connecting me in every direction, including through time—which is, after all, a fluid construct.

———

As if we didn't already know it, COVID-19 drove home the point that we have limited control over our circumstances. But we can begin to train the mind to control our responses. Emerging from a place of calm, a deeper pool, that response might not only be care of self, but also care of others: action.

Here's how my small portion of this *nidra* script ends: The waves throw droplets into the air where they sparkle and vanish. The sky is reflected in the water. The sky is so blue, and it is boundless. It is boundless.

DAWN RAFFEL is the author of five books, most recently *The Strange Case of Dr. Couney: How a Mysterious European Showman Saved Thousands of American Babies*. She also teaches yoga and creative writing.

RECIPE FOR CONNECTION

By Jennifer Rosner

My mother, a flitting hummingbird, calms once her sauté pans are simmering on the stove. Five feet tall, ninety pounds, she moves about her kitchen with an assuredness she doesn't have in other domains.

Her world started shrinking before the virus hit. At age eighty-nine, she lost her husband of sixty-three years (my beloved father). Her therapy practice dwindled considerably. She refrained from most driving and retreated from friends. Thankfully, she didn't live alone. My sister and nephew shared the Connecticut split-level, though their lives were busy. Most days, my mother's focus was on cooking the evening's dinner: Salmon with tomatoes, capers, and olives. Tagliatelle with zucchini and lemon. She took pride in her culinary works.

When the virus began ravaging New York City, my brother and his family fled to my mother's house. With them came boxes of cleaning supplies, canned foods, crackers—and intense anxiety. They were particularly concerned with how my mother washed her hands: not often enough, not with the proper soap, not for twenty seconds. They fervently objected whenever she prepared food. Though she stayed home and was the most vulnerable of the bunch, they skipped her elaborate dinners and prepared their own food. In phone calls, my sister reported my mother's further retreat: she was spending most of her time in her bedroom, far from the kitchen.

Meanwhile, in my house several hours away, I was quarantined with my husband and two children. There was a lot of food prep. One afternoon, I called my mother to ask her advice about a recipe. Should

I use sun-dried or fresh tomatoes for a Mediterranean chicken dish I was attempting? My mother perked up and gave me several tips: add paprika to the dredging flour; use ghee in addition to olive oil.

She called me the following day to ask how the dish turned out, and what I was making that night. Honestly, I was flailing. My eldest daughter had celiac and a long list of food allergies, and our now limited supermarket trips made meal preparation even more challenging. My mother brainstormed options with me. What about fish with roasted tomatoes and potatoes? Steak marinated in a raspberry vinaigrette?

Food wasn't always simple between us. As a semi-recovered anorexic, my mother kept an eagle eye on what I ate when I was a child. She made cooking an event back then too, yet she barely ate anything. My eating stressed her out. The intervening years have softened her, and my daughter's growth issues refocused my thoughts on food intake (for optimal nourishment, not weight). My mother's specially-made foods—raspberry popovers, crunchy maple sweet potatoes, caramelized pear pie—manage to bring me comfort and trigger only the mildest hints of past craziness. My kids love these same foods, with particular adaptations.

Now, while sheltering in place, my mother and I have a daily cooking call. She advises me on what I aim to make for dinner, offering ideas I'd never think of. Last night, with her encouragement, I pulled off a pasta with roasted cauliflower and hazelnuts. Who knew that adding a bit of pasta water could help thicken a sauce? I can't wait to tell her how tasty it was, and to hear her pleasure in it.

We're eating better than we ever would have, and I believe my mother is less lonely, as a result of our calls. When we hang up, I picture her rifling through the pages of well-worn cookbooks, considering what to suggest to me for tomorrow's family dinner.

My sister reports that our mother has reasserted herself in her kitchen. After she speaks to me (yes, ginger *will* help the dressing), she sets her pans on the stove and conjures what she can from her pantry. Though my brother and his family continue to eat their own food at different shifts, my sister and nephew gladly eat whatever she cooks.

I have not set eyes on my mother for eight weeks. She will turn ninety this July, and I hope that, by then, we will be able to safely visit in person. For now, we're in touch by phone, me standing at my kitchen counter, she fluttering around hers. Both looking forward to a day when we'll cook an elaborate meal, and eat it, together.

JENNIFER ROSNER's writing has appeared in the *New York Times, The Massachusetts Review,* and elsewhere. She is the author of four books, including her debut novel, *The Yellow Bird Sings.*

STRANGE CURRENCY

By Sandra Sarr

I miss pushing my cart down aisles,
pressing ridged flesh of avocados,
sensing its dead-on resistance
under my thumb. And plucking tomatoes,
their weight cupped in my palms.

Now, Chelsie, a stranger
on a screen, delivers to my house,
which she and Siri found.
I glimpse her from the door,
porch light on, watch the masked

figure off-load bag after bag
ahead of a storm I'd warned
of when she texted from the store
asking if a strange brand would suffice
as ample replacement. She lugs

a sack of dog food to last a month,
plus six bottles of pinot noir, forbidden
by Instacart, but offered and purchased
separately by Chelsie,
repaid by me.

How does one repay a stranger
who delivers at 9 o'clock at night,
just 40 minutes after I click on pictures

195

of items a stranger's hands
put in a cart, then in her Nissan,

then on my porch, no hello or goodbye?
Inside, I unload the goods, gloved,
cautious. Behold: two avocados
Chelsie hand chose for me.
A ripeness test—giving or rigid—

I squeeze the flesh and am met
with that familiar resistance.
Thunderclaps rattle my house,
lightning strobes our sky.
Is Chelsie pulling up to her house,

wipers flapping, mask draped at her
neck, safe? Or is she steering back to Albert-
sons, Winn Dixie, Trader Joe's? Who
waits for Chelsie at home as she
fills the needs of strangers?

I lift my phone and up
her tip, the most generous I can afford.
Popping a cork on a pinot she made
possible, I pour a glass for one,
quarantined in a new city, solitary,

except for strangers venturing
forth so that I, just recovered
from another life-snatcher, cancer,
can up my chance of seeing another year.

What currency compensates

these acts of compassion
amid the twin infection
of virus and poverty
that thrusts us into a swirl
of mutual need?

SANDRA SARR is a writer and poet living in Baton Rouge, Louisiana. She is currently revising her debut novel, *The Road to Indigo*.

IN THE ABSENCE OF OTHERS

By Steve Yarbrough

My wife and I live in a small town a few miles north of Boston. In the summer of 2016, a family of three moved in across the street, and when I saw the guy remove a guitar and mandolin from their car, it seemed too good to be true.

I started playing country music and bluegrass when I was about nine, and by the age of twelve was playing in a country combo with the local soil conservation agent and a high school football coach. For many years, though, I'd seldom had anyone to play with. The absence of others had left me listening too much to myself. I tried to keep the melody going with a flat pick while still strumming chords, so I never really attempted to stretch out and develop my solo skills. Furthermore, I have no vocal range and so mostly just hummed rather than trying to learn songs. Every now and then, I'd get disgusted and quit playing. When you do that, you lose your calluses, making the return to playing steel-stringed instruments painful for both the ears and the fingers.

I wasted no time going over and introducing myself to Edmund Jorgensen and his wife and small son. I told him I'd seen the guitar and mandolin, and he said he played those and several other instruments but was no virtuoso. I didn't propose playing then, for two reasons. The first was that if he played guitar and mandolin, there was a fair chance that, like me, he'd be drawn to bluegrass—and bluegrass musicians, with some very notable exceptions, tend to be conservatives, sometimes inhabiting the far-right fringes. In that politically charged summer, I wanted no contact with anyone of that ilk. But I checked him out and discovered that while he worked in the tech sector, he had a classics degree from Boston University and had also published a couple of well-received speculative novels. The reviews I found online made it seem highly unlikely that his closet contained a MAGA cap.

The other reason I didn't suggest we play was that a couple of times, I'd made a fool of myself trying to play with better musicians. Bluegrass flatpicking is an intricate operation heavily dependent on alternate pick strokes. Once you play a downstroke when you should be playing an upstroke, or vice-versa, it's almost impossible to recover. I had often read from my novels in front of some of the best writers in the world and never felt flustered. Fall apart in a bluegrass jam, though, and my face would turn bright red, my throat would constrict, and as soon as possible I'd lay my guitar in the case and slink away.

On a warm but windless afternoon, I picked up a guitar to play for an hour or so before dinner. I noticed that across the street, the neighbors' windows were open. Without giving myself much time to think about it, I opened mine too, then sat down and started playing "Wildwood Flower."

A few days later, Edmund called and said, "Hey, we ought to play sometime. But I'm not as good as you are. I heard you the other day." His recollection is that he had to ask me several times before I agreed.

It immediately became clear that we were not coming from quite the same musical universe. For some years he had been playing in a blues band with his father, who performed professionally in the '60s and '70s, opening for John Sebastian and the Lovin' Spoonful. In the blues band, Edmund is the pianist. As a guitarist, he was strictly a folky fingerpicker, but he also played Celtic music on the mandolin. Though my listening tastes are eclectic, I could not play anything but bluegrass and country and some rudimentary blues. Until a year or so earlier, I could not fingerpick at all.

Those first few times we played, we didn't set the world on fire. But eventually, because many old-time or bluegrass fiddle tunes have Celtic cousins, we found common ground in pieces like "Soldier's Joy." Initially, I played guitar and he played mandolin, though occasionally we switched up. He has a good voice, and he usually did the vocals. It also turned out he'd written some really fine songs. Garrison Keillor once told Gillian Welch and David Rawlings, "Your new songs sound so old," and the same could be said of Edmund's.

Playing together became a regular thing. We'd work on a tune for a few sessions, then record it and post it on YouTube and Facebook. After a while we developed a bit of a following there, having dubbed ourselves The Harrison Street Two. This past January, shortly after the virus outbreak, we made our initial public appearance, playing a well-received charity concert in Waltham. We began making plans to do a number of other events in spring around Boston.

———

Some years ago, before meeting Edmund, I composed an instrumental, one of only two that I can claim to have "written." According to another musician friend of mine, it could have been titled "Stephen Foster Meets Norman Blake," since it bears melodic resemblance to Foster's "Hard Times Come Again No More," as well as Blake's "Last Train from Poor Valley." One of the last few times we got together, Edmund told me he'd written some lyrics for my tune. I quickly fell in love with them.

The Old Dusty Door

In the back of my mind where no one can see
There stands an old dusty door
I keep it shut tight with a lock and a key
And I never go in there any more
But I wake up each day and I love my wife
And I tousle my children's golden hair
Sometimes there's so much sweetness in my life
I almost forget that it's there

Each man is born with a portion of days
His pleasures and his burdens to bear
Set is his path and graven are his ways
Though the yearnings of his heart lay elsewhere
And when it's my hour and death comes on
Like waves breaking soft on the shore
I'll say my farewells and I'll take your hand
And step through that old dusty door

The song would have been included in our spring gigs. But things
dramatically changed. The last time I taught a class before the college
where I work went to distance learning, I came home and found a
message from Edmund: three days before our most recent session, he
had most likely been exposed to the virus. Some days later, I discov-
ered that I had been exposed myself.

Our families went into self-imposed quarantine, but none of us got sick. The close calls led to our rigidly following Governor Charlie Baker's social distancing guidelines, which as of this writing continue to be in force, as our state loses between one hundred twenty-five and two hundred fifty people a day to the virus. Once again, I sit and play guitar and mandolin by myself. Every now and then, I look out the window and see Edmund doing the same thing across the street, working on a tune that we plan to play together one day when hard times—having come again once more, as hard times inevitably do—relinquish their hold on us.

Hard times, we remind ourselves, never last forever.

STEVE YARBROUGH is the author of eleven books, most recently *The Unmade World*. He lives with his wife, the Polish essayist Ewa Hryniewicz-Yarbrough, in Stoneham, Massachusetts.

THE INESCAPABLE JOYS OF MOTHERHOOD

By Kristen Millares Young

I am lying flat on my back in a tent in my yard. Built for six people, with the rain fly it covers the flagstone patio we installed when we couldn't imagine wanting a lawn.

In the quiet of early morning, my husband's phone lights up the crags on his face. I ask for the time. "Three forty-five," he whispers, our sons sleeping around us.

I am awake. There is no acceptable remedy for that truth.

It is week six of our family's self-quarantine. For reasons I don't entirely understand, but having to do with the pandemic during which my husband and I have been overburdened with work while home-schooling our preschooler and kindergartener, we have left our property very few times. There is a big park just two blocks away.

The first weekend, we drove to a remote rural county park called Guillemot Cove, where we kept a safe social distance from other skittish people in search of an easy hike with a big view. We sprayed our hands with sanitizer before eating our packaged picnic on an oyster beach, saltwater lapping the driftwood shores from where we sat to the foot of a snowy mountain range.

The second time—Was it last week? Or two weeks ago?—we walked down to Lake Washington, about a half mile away, during which time I counted dozens of opportunities for infection. I don't like thinking this way. But my boys are four and six years old, and, to be frank, they don't always remember to do what I tell them. It's hard to adapt to these new circumstances. The news brings fresh and hellish revelations by the minute about just how easy it is to contract the virus from surfaces or passersby. I search the news for key words like *slipstream*.

We were masked with bandannas and hats and ski gaiters pulled up past our noses but (goddammit, Kristen) no gloves. (Why didn't you get the gloves? Is it really that hard to get out the door with two kids and snacks? Yes.) Even though I've told them repeatedly not to touch anything, the first thing they do, after we pause to exchange loud greetings with neighbors across the street, is push the crosswalk button. "No! No! Boys! I said no!" I pull from my bag the last tube of antibacterial wipes we scored before our panicked populace bought up the world.

At this point we are crossing the street. Really, that's what we need to be focused on, but I worry that they may touch their nostrils suck their fingers wipe a crust from their eyes before we reach the curb—these are not idle fears—and so I am wiping their hands as we cross, the kind of frantic multitasking that invites judgment from waiting drivers. But we get there.

I am trying to keep them safe. The only thing that matters to me, right now, as a mother, is that we survive this thing together, and in good spirits if we can manage it. And that is what astounds me. We are improbably happy.

I brought snacks for bribes, the kind of packaged pretend-food I would never stock but which was clicked on by my husband, who in his mercy provides small treats for us, rather than the siege-like deprivation I might broker were I in charge of groceries. He knows better by now. My frugality is in the marrow, instilled in me by my *abuela*, just passed, who should have been a nun but instead became a matriarch. She was my guide star, that impossible woman.

She also had a tendency to stay where she was planted. An exile born to a first generation, she became a first generation before birthing a first generation who made her own first generation. Aside from those big moves—one country per generation, not counting all the interstitial places from Lalín to Havana to Cueto to Orange to Miami to Tampa to Seattle—she stayed put so much that I began to fear she had a phobia not unlike her fear of the death which claimed her, which will claim us all.

What I mean to say is that she barely left the house unless she was brought somewhere. Writing this essay revealed an intergenerational pattern that, though reinforced by gubernatorial decree, still distressed me so much that I rose from my laptop at 10 a.m. on a work day to demand a family walk just when my children were happily ensconced on the couch with their brand-new tablets, performing educational app tasks to unlock Minecraft, the worldbuilding education they prefer, for which it would be hypocritical for me as a novelist to scold them.

On the path to the lake, one particular woman won't move off her dry side of the marshy path, so my family of four, looking like bandits in bandannas since our infrequent outings didn't seem to require proper masks, circles her orbit as one. The meadow mud will flake off their shoes for days once we get home. Part of me cheers for her – older, alone and resolute. The other part of me wants to give her a look which to do properly would require lowering my bandanna.

At the lake shore, ducks paddle near with soft quacks, hopeful but not begging, and I pivot that moment of beauty to instruct our boys about showy male and drab female patterning, a biological evolution whose fractals are belied by the fact that their dad wears hoodies and I, makeup. My sons squint against unaccustomed sun and ask for another Oreo. Turtles pile up along the silvered root of a partly-immersed snag. Are they mating? I, too, squint, but learn little more about the wildlife of Rainier Valley, where a week later I regard the sky through the tent's door flap.

I am losing track of time.

———

Yesterday, I scooped my cat's excesses from every nook of my garden using a trowel and a dustbin. I have never been much of a gardener, preferring perennials and pioneers over plants that require my seasonal attention, but my blueberries are trimmed and greening, and it looks to be another good year for the thorny gooseberries I should have planted in the corner of the yard, rather than by the car.

The boys rocket around our basement, swinging from wooden hoops that my husband installed to dangle from its ceiling, through which their raucous shouts emanate into the living room, where my husband is helping to salvage our state's economy, one email and Zoom call at a time. From the office, which I've claimed for ten years because I work from home, I write standing up. When I can be reasonably assured of their safety, I wear earbuds that pipe in brown noise to cover the hubbub of my beloveds.

I'll be fair with myself. I have worked hard every day of the pandemic. I had to. I've been in a frenzy of rescheduling the book tour for my debut novel *Subduction*, more than a decade in the making.

Magical thinking. I don't believe I'll be flying to California in July or September, but I had to make plans, just in case. Belief is a tricky thing. It can sustain you through hard times and tank you during the good.

In preparation to write this essay, I spent more time outdoors with my kids. Cataloguing our mandated absence from the outside world spooked me into a deeper engagement. Such are the revelations of literature and its reckonings. I have been trying so hard to enact a vision I built for my life before the pandemic. I have been counting on their love. Their forgiveness and forgetting. And my own.

KRISTEN MILLARES YOUNG is a prize-winning investigative journalist, book critic, and essayist who serves as prose writer-in-residence at Hugo House in Seattle. Her debut novel is *Subduction*.

WHAT TO BRING TO A DIE-IN

By Amber Flame

leave: bring:

security blanket   bulletproof vest

inescapable skin   reliable witnesses (white)

tongue   choking throat

justification   guns

and if not your guns, then your wide screaming mouths
and if not your screaming mouths, then your gasping tears
and if not your tears, then your fist clenched in anger
and if not your fist, then your hands raised in surrender.

bring your own body
pulsing; add the heat of your children.
the ones still left living. lay down.
be empty. silent. become the ideal
image of you. don't _____.

brace for impact.
expect them to shoot.

AMBER FLAME is a writer, composer, and performer, whose work has garnered artistic merit residencies with Hedgebrook, Vermont Studio Center, and more. Flame served as the 2017-2019 poetry writer-in-residence at Hugo House in Seattle, and is a queer Black single mama just one magic trick away from growing her unicorn horn.

ON ASKING MAMA TO PRAY FOR ME

By teri elam

that my fingers are places of prayer
—Lucille Clifton

At ninety-two, Mama no longer bends down. Knees twice-oper-
ated on, the last time barely making it through. When she rises—later
each day than before, it seems—she twists her dwindling body, bones
now prominent, neck stubborn, craned as if ready to pray. I'd lay my
gloriously thick, nappy head of hair onto that same neck, burrow into
her lap after a fall, skinned knee, or hurt feelings. She'd wrap her hick-
ory arms around my scrawny, barely-there version of her own self. I'd
not move a limb until she kissed the injury I pointed to and sang in
her North Carolina lilt, "God bless Mama's baby." Then she'd push me
back into the world again.

These days she stays in place. Her feet, having walked, run, pounded
a billion steps, warily touch the ground, finding security in her gold
Daniel Greens. From the side of the bed, her "Hallelujah! Hallelujah
Lawd's!" flow full-throated, as if coming from the ten-year-old body
baptized in a creek off Pamlico River eighty-two years before. That's
when she first gave herself over to God. The same year her mother,
called Air by most, disappeared into the night-wind to escape batter-
ing fists, leaving Mama behind to care for herself and all else. Still, she
kneeled down every day; I imagine praying for the return of Air's neck
when she felt injured, each day her body becoming its own mother.

My body is cranky and, at times, willful, but its limbs will bend into a shape or two, with a wince. My body arrogantly redesigns itself without my permission. I have not yet walked, run, or pounded half the steps of my mother. And yet I have no good excuse for why it does not often lay itself down to pray, except when it can't catch its own breath or feel its limbs. On our morning talks, Mama asks if I've read *The Daily Word*, the devotional she mails me religiously, my name and address etched meticulously in shaky cursive, a skeleton of her once teacher-perfect penmanship. This is 2020's version of my formerly thick, still nappy head resting on her craned neck. Maybe sensing, in my hesitation, a white lie forming, she whispers, "Is death your God?" "Sometimes, right now," I feel like saying as I watch increasing fatalities scrawl across the bottom of MSNBC, but I don't. What I say instead is what I often do when my adult self is afraid, injured, or feeling skinned, "Mama, please pray for me—for us all."

During our last visit, me in my car, she at her door, the world locked up around us, smiles and grimaces masked and touch a distant hope, I ask her again for her prayers. She stretches out her right hand, fingers wrinkled, hand trembling slightly as she steadies herself. She speaks. I hear her North Carolina lilt flow again, slowly, sure and full-throated, "God bless Mama's baby." This time, she pauses and adds, "Pray for yourselves, too, my love." And with an air kiss and a wave goodbye, she pushes me—she pushes us all—back into the world again.

TERI ELAM is a writer, leadership coach, and human resources professional in Atlanta. Her recent work can be found in *Slice Magazine*, *Auburn Avenue*, *Prairie Schooner*, and as a short film for the *Visual Poetry Project*.

PART FIVE: AND DO NOT STOP

IN CONVERSATION WITH
LUIS ALBERTO URREA

"Write your story across the sky..."

I first heard Luis Alberto Urrea speak at Hugo House in Seattle, in 2015, to a rapt room of about three hundred people. He talked about stories, essays, and poems as growing things, words on pages like leaves on high branches, colorful and fluttering in the wind. He talked about the understory: the roots below ground, the mysterious lower depths that nourish these branches. I remember him saying that it takes trust and intuition, and a lot of digging around in the dirt, to uncover the true essence of the story you want to convey. His own stories, fiction and nonfiction, are exquisitely crafted portrayals of how the spirit is capable of soaring above the pain, fear, and fragility inherent in being human.

I sought out Luis to poke a shovel in the ground and search for an understory of the pandemic. What is the essence of this story we are all living?

Jennifer Haupt: *In 2018, you told Krista Tippett that a deep truth of our time is "we miss each other. We have this drive to erect barriers between ourselves, and yet this also makes us a little crazy." You were talking about the U.S.-Mexico border. What opportunity does the pandemic offer for us to come together, with compassion?*

LAU: I was recently on one of those dreaded Zoom chat sessions that we have now in lieu of panels, readings, and lectures. It was Pam

Houston, Joe Wilkins, and me. We ended up talking about the unexpected blessing that may come from this plague: tenderness. Clearly, those fellows standing in front of city halls demanding the right to not wear masks while brandishing machine guns are not about to have a satori-like moment of spiritual illumination. But I think the vast majority of people out there have been forced into a kind of meditative state.

You can see it in social media feeds. I see writers and artists creating spaces for others to connect, to create, to share, to workshop. I accidently launched one myself on my Facebook page that has gone on for more than fifty posts, with people sharing more than twelve thousand beautiful images from their lives. It was an instant community. Guess what—out of all of those postings there has not been one snarky, mean-spirited, politicized attack. Never.

Clearly, something is stirring in our hearts. We are hurt and damaged and yearning for our better selves, desperately dreaming of a kinder world in the days to come. Will we forget that when we can all go back to our concerts and football games and fancy restaurants and bars? I don't know. But one must, in the words of Brennan Manning, have ruthless trust.

JH: *It seems that the crisis of the pandemic has pushed us to a crossroads of caring, of choosing the deeper compassion and becoming "us," or reacting out of fear and becoming even more deeply divided.*

LAU: This is exactly what's happening. I think it's funny that super tough guys are in a seeming panic and all of us snowflakes are taking positive actions, thinking, planning, sharing, creating. One part of our national community is panic-buying toilet paper, making sure their survival bunkers are full of freeze-dried food packs. Another part is planting gardens, making masks, dropping supplies at neighbors' houses. (By the way, at our house, we don't have any freeze-dried food. But it looks like a killer crop of tomatoes and strawberries may be on its way!)

I'm trying to see the in-between. It can't just be one thing or the other. It can't be all isolation or all connection, all grief or all love, all self-concern or all concern for others. Finding a path forward is going to take the courage to be creative instead of the obsession with being "right." The answer lies somewhere we don't yet see, but we have to get there. I'm looking for the possibilities.

JH: What do you see as the best possible outcome we might achieve, as individuals and as a society, from this devastating time?

LAU: Let me begin this answer metaphorically: the earth, like writers and poets, speaks to us in images. Have you noticed that once we retreated from our throne of world dominance, most of us went home and closed the door? And physical things began to change on the planet. It reminds me of the Aymara bishop from Bolivia I once knew, who explained that during communion, his church's tradition is to pour wine and drop the first wafer on the ground. They know the earth as La Pachamama, and what child doesn't feed their mother first?

As soon as we were forced to stop our continual tantrum of consumption and aggression, the canals cleared up in Venice, animals came back to walk up and down city streets, pollution levels dropped all over the world. We moved to save ourselves and withdrew from the world. And La Pachamama kicked it into overdrive to try to make the most of the change. You can feel the hope for the future in the changes of the earth around us. Who is not seeing more birds in their backyards, feeling more of the wind through the trees?

The reality as I see it now—politically speaking, culturally speaking—is very similar. We are going to come out of our dens soon to a planet that is trying to heal itself. But also into a body politic that has gotten tangled and confused and toxic in the extreme. We should learn from what is happening around us: Our destiny is in our hands. We changed our lives because we didn't want to die. But now we need to work together for other changes because we want to live. That tenderness I mentioned earlier, I think, is this looming sense of connectedness. We were all equalized, all of us shared the same experience. Watching videos of other abandoned cities, closed landmarks, people waving from balconies all over the world, brings us all to tears every time because we are in this together. And I think that connectedness scares the hell out of those in power.

People are going to want change. It has to be more about each other than about a toxic need to build a monument to ourselves. I think we will need to honor the deep feeling that we are building a monument to each other. As I've always said, there is no them, there is only us.

Building this new world for *us* is not a passive thing: *You* have to march out into the sunlight and grab that power and carry it where you need it to go. Light the torch to knock back the night. Don't sit back. Take action, exercise your voice. Yes, vote, of course, and make sure everyone around you votes. But we have stayed home for each other. We literally stopped our worlds for each other. Now it's time to get your ass outside and live for each other. Sing and do not stop. March and do not stop. Work and do not stop. Write your story across the sky and don't despair because despair is the most powerful weapon of the dominant. It will only make you weary and, ultimately, afraid to stand in the light.

A finalist for the Pulitzer Prize for his landmark work of nonfiction *The Devil's Highway*, Luis Alberto Urrea is the author of seventeen books of fiction, nonfiction, and poetry. A Guggenheim Fellow, Urrea is a Distinguished Professor of creative writing at the University of Illinois-Chicago.

AMERICA THE BEAUTIFUL AGAIN

By Richard Blanco

How I sang *O, beautiful* like a psalm at church
with my mother, her Cuban accent scaling-up
every vowel: *O, bee-yoo-tee-ful*, yet in perfect
pitch, delicate and tuned to the radiant beams
of stained glass light. How she taught me to fix
my eyes on the crucifix as we sang our thanks
to our savior for this country that saved us—
our voices hymns as passionate as the organ
piping towards the very heavens. How I sang
for spacious skies closer to those skies while
perched on my father's sun-beat shoulders,
towering above our first Fourth of July parade.
How the timbre through our bodies mingled,
breathing, singing as one with the brass notes
of the marching band playing the only song
he ever learned in English. How I dared sing it
at assembly with my teenage voice cracking
for amber waves of grain that I'd never seen,
nor the *purple mountain majesties*—but could
imagine them in each verse rising from my gut,
every exclamation of praise I belted out until
my throat hurt: *America!* and again *America!*
How I began to read Nietzsche and doubt god,
yet still wished for god to *shed His grace on
thee, and crown thy good with brotherhood.*
How I still want to sing despite all the truth
of our wars and our gunshots ringing louder

218

than our school bells, our politicians smiling
lies at the mic, the deadlock of our divided
voices shouting over each other instead of
singing together. How I want to sing again—
beautiful or not, just to be harmony—*from
sea to shining sea*—with the only country
I know enough to know how to sing for.

RICHARD BLANCO was selected by President Obama as the fifth
inaugural poet in U.S. history. He is the youngest and the first Latino,
immigrant, and gay person to serve in such a role. His latest book of
poems is *How to Love a Country*.

STAMINA
(MEMORIAL DAY WEEKEND, 2020)

By Pam Houston

A lamb was born here on Saturday, a little ram, and when I say little, I mean it. He was a preemie, born late in the spring, conceived a month after the usual end of mating season.

The last thing we need around here is another ram. We have two already, and though they are best friends, they spend most of their time with the tops of their heads grotesquely bloodied, doing to each other exactly as their name suggests. Sometimes, for fun, they ram me, taking me down from behind at the knees.

These are Icelandic sheep, which are, any shearer will confirm, the wildest of the domestic breeds. The rams have large circular horns, big enough to do some damage. My Icelandics have fought off coyotes, a mountain lion, and a black bear, and though some of them lost the battle, some of them, including Elsie, the mother of this little preemie, won. Which is why she is alive to birth another ram, which as I mentioned, is the last thing we need. It is the ewes who protect the herd from predators, while the rams, the ones with the great big horns, cower in the back. It is also the ewes who protect their babies from the very rams who sired them. I have seen a ram toss a newborn into the air minutes after birth. Luckily, lambs bounce.

The ranchers in this valley will tell you it is only the male lambs the rams go after, in order to cut down competition, but I have seen a ram lift a tiny, mewling female into the air likewise, and as I was running to separate them, I have seen the ewe—five minutes postpartum—pin that ram, who weighs a third again as much as she does, to the ground.

Saturday's lamb was the tiniest ever, and more than a little listless. Not eager to nurse. Icelandics always give birth midmorning, so the baby has the maximum hours of warmth and daylight to get steady on his feet and well fed. Over the course of the long afternoon I prompted the little ram to nurse successfully at least twice, but Elsie wasn't doing much to encourage him, which made me think she had already given him up for dead. There is always the thought, when a ewe shows little interest, that she might know more than I do, might know the lamb has some genetic defect, or that one of his internal systems isn't right.

I live at high altitude, so even this far into May the temperature was forecast to dip into the low twenties. After nightfall, Elsie wasn't even trying to keep the little ram warm and he was too out of it to seek comfort himself. I bundled up in my fleece lined pants, my down parka and wool hat, to sleep in the barn with Elsie and her baby. Why didn't I take the baby into the warm house with me? I was still hoping Elsie wouldn't reject him outright. Bottle babies are a lot of fun, but they rarely get the nutrition and antibodies they need to thrive.

What you learn on a ranch is that the sweetest things die, and there are few things in the world sweeter than the tight tight curls of a newborn Icelandic sheep or the warm breath that rises up and out of him, or when he licks your chin with his tiny pink tongue. A year from now, should this baby live, he will be big and strong enough to break my kneecaps, but this summer, he will bound around the pasture chasing butterflies, baa-ing his sweet high-pitched baa, and tumbling through the grass with his older girl cousins.

Most of my neighbors would tell you I had already gone too far trying to save him, that I should always let nature take its course. But I am not a rancher. I am a writer, a teacher, a progressive, an activist, a woman who raises Icelandic sheep and names them. COVID-19 has kept me home for three solid months and connected me more intensely than ever to my animals. Sleeping in the barn with the preemie feels like a natural extension of all that.

Elsie bedded down away from the lamb. I lowered myself to the ground with my back against a haystack and pulled the baby onto my lap. He snuggled into my down jacket, making little sucking sounds. Every time he wanted up, I let him, but then he would just stand there, staring at the wall and swaying, so I would scoop him back up and he'd bed down again. At first light I got him to nurse a little, but Elsie wouldn't stand still long enough for him to get much milk. By 8 a.m. he had lost the use of his back legs, and was shaking no matter how tight I held him, a sure sign he was starving to death.

There is no substitute for authentic ewe's milk, but I went to the house and mixed up some Sav-a-Lam milk replacer. The baby was too weak to suck, too weak, by then, to care, so I force-fed him, not with a tube, just with a bottle. I forced the nipple in his mouth and rubbed his throat to make him swallow and didn't let him out of my lap until two ounces of the milk was gone.

With newborns, if you are going to see improvement with milk replacer, you usually see it quickly. I wasn't seeing much. He had stopped shaking but his eyes were dull and he was still unwilling to stand. By that time I'd decided if he was going to die, I could give him some comfort while he did it. I rocked him and kissed his lanolin-smelling head, his sweet little nubbins of horns. He weighed almost nothing.

Elsie watched me, a little coldly, I thought, from her corner of the enclosure. What do you know that I don't know? I asked her, but she just chewed her cud.

I didn't know what was wrong with the little ram, but I did know that one hundred thousand Americans would be dead from COVID-19 by the end of the weekend. I knew the real number was actually higher, because several states (Florida, Georgia, Texas) had been cooking their COVID-19 books. I knew the vast majority of the dead, grandmothers and grandfathers, husbands and wives, doctors and nurses, daughters and sons, had died without their loved ones there beside them, and I knew tens of thousands of those deaths were unnecessary, due only to the colossal failure—perhaps intentional—of the Trump administration and its enablers in the GOP. I knew our government was being deliberately dismantled from within. I knew that by virtue of being an outspoken woman I was no longer safe here, at my beloved ranch, and I also knew that on the scale of who is and is not safe in this country, I fared infinitely better than most. I knew that it was long past time for those selfish and shameful men to relinquish control of this country into the hands of women. I knew it was time for women to step into the power they have been gaslighted out of believing was theirs all along. I knew I had some role in that, that perhaps we all did, and I knew I needed to figure out what it was.

I spent all day Sunday in the barn, and force-fed that little ram six more times, two ounces every two hours. He got so sick of me shoving the rubber nipple into his mouth that the seventh time he got up, bobbed and weaved over to Elsie, and started nursing. I spent Sunday night in the barn too, but by then he was toddling around again and Elsie was showing a bit more interest. Mostly he slept curled up against her, coming over to sniff at me once an hour or so, maybe making sure *I* was warm enough.

By Monday morning, it seemed for the first time that the little ram might make it. Before the day was over, a Minneapolis policeman named Derek Chauvin would kneel on the neck of George Floyd for 8 minutes and 46 seconds, killing him dead.

When I was a girl my father broke many things that belonged to me: my femur and my hymen, to name the two most significant. He crumpled sixteen of his cars around my body and his own, driving drunk and careless and angry. Then there was the psychological torture (see any Trump tweet of the last seventy-two hours, of any seventy-two hours) which I still insist was the worst torture of all. Surviving my father's house took hypervigilance and wiliness, the ability to separate my mind from whatever was being done to my body. Most of all it took stamina, seventeen years of it. The drumbeat, always in my head, saying, keep your eyes open, plan for the worst-case scenario, stay alive at any cost, survive long enough to get out.

By first light on Tuesday, the little ram's legs worked perfectly. I spent parts of the next three days and nights in the barn, and then it warmed up enough to send me back to my own bed.

Now he's a week old, skipping across the outdoor enclosure, bouncing off the walls of the stall, crawling all over Elsie and ramming the holy hell out of the water trough. He weighs four times what he did last Saturday, and when I lift him, I feel his warm rounded belly, full. The milk replacer is closed up and put away for next year, and even now, every time he sees me, he runs straight over to Elsie to nurse.

I am not any sort of a hero. I saved the ram because I thought maybe I could. I saved him because none of my heartfelt writing, nor my activism nor my passionate progressive values could save George

Floyd. I saved him because cities are burning all across my country and because a man I can't keep straight anymore from my dead father promised to do this to us, and now he is doing it every day. I saved the lamb to mitigate (if slightly) the wave of grief that is raining down on us, to prove to myself that I have both the strength and the stamina to save at least one small fragile thing.

I left my father's house when I was seventeen, and did not expect to find myself back in it at fifty-eight, along with my 330 million brothers and sisters. To beat COVID-19, to beat these soulless goons whose endgame is always cruelty for cruelty's sake, we are going to have to play the long game, all of us together, even if the men with the big horns cower in the back. I can't run quite as fast as I used to, nor kick quite as hard, but what I haven't lost over the decades is stamina. Sleeping in the barn for a week to save a lamb whose mother left it for dead may not sound like much, but my mother left me for dead too, so often, in my father's bed, and now you ought to see how I can ram a water trough. You ought to see how I still bounce.

Elsie looks at me with a little more respect these days than she used to. In the wilds of Iceland, she might have had to abandon that baby, but here she has a barn full of hay and a woman just tenacious enough to believe she can save anything. Maybe some lives. Maybe democracy. This morning, and only this morning, I named the little ram Tank.

PAM HOUSTON is the author of seven books of fiction and nonfiction including *Deep Creek: Finding Hope in The High Country*, and *Airmail: Letters on Politics, Pandemics, and Place*. She teaches creative writing at UC Davis and the Institute of American Indian Arts and is cofounder and creative director of the literary nonprofit Writing By Writers.

WHY GET OUT OF BED?

By Jennifer Haupt

Why Get Out of Bed?

Because that's what people do; it is the healthy thing to do.

Because I have to pee.

Because there's a sour film on my teeth.

Because I should clip the hangnail on my right index finger.

Because the dog needs to be fed, there's a load of laundry on the bathroom floor—not to mention my job. There is work to be done. It is what is done, even during a pandemic.

Because getting out of bed is the right thing to do; it is the responsible way to live. But what if I did not do the right thing when I opened my eyes in the morning?

Because it's a little scary when I lie in bed and ask myself this question. I imagine there is a choice as I slap the alarm and roll over and wonder: Why? What would happen if I didn't rip back the sheets and slap one foot on the floor and then the other, and then keep on moving all day long?

Because if I decide it's okay to sleep in for an hour or two, then what's to stop me from choosing to sleep until noon, two, dinner time?

Because I might decide to turn on the radio or TV. I might decide that *Judge Judy* and *Oprah* and smelly sheets are preferable to feeding the dog and laundry and sitting at a desk being semi-productive for eight hours. Fuck being responsible.

I mean, really, why haul my ass out of bed in the morning?

Because now I really have to pee and the dog is barking, and this sliver of a nail is digging into the palm of my hand.

Because people will worry. My husband, Eric, will worry and my sons will worry. My dog will just be pissed off. My boss will fire me if I don't show up at the morning Zoom team meeting, maybe not the first day but for sure the next. My friends will think it's just plain creepy if all of my Instagram posts depict a mussed-up, stony-eyed version of me in bed.

Because if I don't get out of bed, then I'm not just suffering from "mild depression" as my therapist writes on the insurance form. *Functional.* That's the key word that defines my well-being.

Because Major Depressive Disorder is defined by inappropriate "sickness behavior." Staying in bed much longer is inappropriate.

Because Eric will come home from work to find me unwashed and watching reruns, eating popcorn and sucking down Dr. Brown's cream soda. Because, I will tell him, today my biggest joy has been the way that the kernels soak up the sugar and melt in my mouth.

Why get out of bed this morning?

Because I hear Eric scooping chow into the dog's bowl.

Because there's the sound of the shower turning off. My son, Drew, is humming as he walks back to his room.

Because there is the release of a pinpoint of pain as I unclench my hand and kick one leg over the edge of the bed.

Because gratitude kicks in as I sit on the toilet and I empty my bladder, and Eric yells down the hall before leaving, "Love ya!"

Because I do have the choice to get out of bed.

JENNIFER HAUPT, editor of *Alone Together*, is the editor/curator of the *Psychology Today* blog, "One True Thing." She is also the author of the novel, *In the Shadow of 10,000 Hills*, and is currently working on an autobiographical novel that takes place in Haiti.

BEYOND ALL THAT

(GABRIEL)

By Christine Hemp

I squeeze myself into Time. It's tight
like a little coat or a skin I'm much too big for.
I do it, though, for Spaciousness—for the Light

I bring with me. Her eyes at first blink with tears,
her pupils wide, and in them I can see the door
of history: the tree she springs from—the sheer

audacity of that branch growing beyond her womb
into memory, blood, and bone. Before
I raise my hand I cannot help but see a tomb

as well; it's why I'm here: That gyre
of Time. Prepositions cannot explain or
place the where or when of that Fire

who sent me. It's all a gift, and what I bring
has no relation to being good, that poor
imitation of love. Horns, halos, or even wings

are not my story, though there are those who
try to make it so: Me on the immaculate floor
holding a white lily I am said to carry through

the corridors of temples, famous paintings.
But she sees beyond all that. At her core
she's at home within her flesh, sustaining

calm when the spark ignites. She holds her belly,
opens her mouth. I tell her something more
about the seed, the fruit. All she does is stare at me.

In our brief exchange, I taste her fear,
but she does not flinch. "Yes," she says. (*Lord,*
how much joy and sorrow can a human bear?)

CHRISTINE HEMP has aired her poetry and essays on NPR, and a
poem of hers has traveled over a billion miles on a NASA mission to
monitor the prenatal activity of stars. She is the author of *That Fall*
(poems) and *Wild Ride Home: Love, Loss and a Little White Horse, a
Family Memoir.*

POSTCARD FROM NEW YORK

By Sally Koslow

Except for the nightly bang-on-a-can salute to healthcare heroes, my city has quieted. Inside, robocalls for timeshares in the Poconos no longer ring every twenty minutes. The weather is warming, but buzzy sidewalk dining is on pause, no clinking glasses or laughter of contented customers. The speech of people out and about is muted, given that they're masked like *banditos*. So few cars drive down the street they have no need to honk, nor do their ear-piercing alarms jolt awake the neighborhood, which, based on unscientific research, is half vacated, with spooked residents sheltering in cottages and condos from Kennebunkport to Key West.

My husband and I have stuck around. New York City is where we want to be. We take precautions, of course. So far, our sanity is intact, and now that ambulance sirens have begun to wail a bit less often, we hear hourly chimes from the stubby bell tower of a nearby church. The tolling reminds me that time is passing. Slowly. Very slowly.

Like many of the city's fan girls, I am not a born New Yorker. When I graduated from a Midwestern university loud with protest, I wanted bright lights and a chance to exercise my writing chops. I flirted with a move to Kansas City to create doggerel for Hallmark or to Washington, DC, for work on the Hill. An ad agency in Minneapolis was also an option, and a lot closer to my home of Fargo. Soon enough, however, I recognized I wanted not simply a city, but *The City*. Though Kansas City, Washington, and Minneapolis were fine places to build a life, New York—a home to all—was calling my name.

If you can make it here . . . Well, you know.

My relocation fell in place as if *bashert*. ("Destined." In New York City, even Southern Baptists spout Yiddish.) I immediately lined up a job at *Mademoiselle*, though I was too much the naïf to realize that many employees at Condé Nast, the magazine's parent company, had trust funds. With equal speed, I found an apartment on the Upper West Side, off Central Park West. That the neighborhood was infested with junkies and I would have been safer at the Barbizon Hotel for Women I also did not know, and my parents back in North Dakota were equally clueless. But ignorance, if not always bliss, can be its own reward, and my Manhattan life took. I married, raised two sons, and climbed several magazines' mastheads, where I enjoyed the view from the top.

Throughout, I stayed in the same neighborhood, which morphed into desirability, thanks to stately pre-World War II buildings and brackets of increasingly lush parks. I, too, evolved. I became another fast-talking New Yorker, always in a rush, one more sardine packed into a subway, which —call me crazy—I loved, since I could read while zipping fifty blocks in ten minutes. After magazines started to wither, I began to write books, the quintessential New York occupation. With a writing workshop, two book clubs, barre and Pilates classes, parks for running and little grandchildren to hug across the river in Brooklyn, life has been pretty sweet.

Enter pandemic. You don't need to be an oracle to predict that when the New York City all-clear signal sounds, like a colossal shofar ending Yom Kippur, life here won't look the same. Many of the shops and restaurants will be shuttered, and massive shortfalls in the budgets of cultural institutions I've taken for granted will bring changes I don't want to imagine. Some of my friends and neighbors who've ditched the city won't return, fearful of cramming back into a dense urban environment. Nor do they want to pay big-ticket real estate fees for a city not fully up to speed.

I, however, don't see myself fleeing. I've tried to imagine Plan B. I'm coming up blank.

Thanks to COVID-19 warnings and my own adult sons, I'm reminded *ad nauseum* that not only am I not so young, I'm suddenly *elderly*. Moreover, my neighborhood, which has a large proportion of residents over sixty, has become known by sociologists as a NORC, a naturally occurring retirement community. People like me are aging in place, a term that has started to feel far too literal as each day melts into the next, punctuated by no-bullshit briefings from our governor. *We're New York tough*, Andrew Cuomo reminds us, and while he adds other adjectives—smart, resourceful, kind, loving—*tough* is the rallying cry.

Tough might be the last attribute I—or any woman—might have hoped someone would attach to me. But tough I will have to be if I'm going to stick around after we're sprung from lockdown and there's more to do than bake another banana bread, read another chapter, watch another episode, or write another page. While you won't find me on a subway again till there's a vaccine, I'll continue to roam this fine city, because, dammit, I love New York.

SALLY KOSLOW is the author of six books, including the international bestseller *The Late, Lamented Molly Marx* and, most recently, the bionovel *Another Side of Paradise*.

DON'T STOP BELIEVIN'

By Shana Mahaffey

One foggy Saturday morning, my husband and I were on our way to deliver food to seniors for the San Francisco Food Bank. We'd never done this before, but then the pandemic has prompted a lot of us to do things we've never done before. As we merged onto the 101 freeway, the unmistakable piano refrain of Journey's "Don't Stop Believin'" filled the car. The song was once an anthem for the San Francisco Giants, played during the eighth inning when they were tied or behind.

"I've never seen the 101 this empty," said Alan. Before the virus he'd been forced to leave our house before 6 a.m. to commute to San Jose. Leaving an hour later meant sitting in traffic.

As we drove toward Potrero Hill and the food bank, I looked back at Oracle Park, the ballpark still called AT&T Park by the locals. The last time I saw the Giants play there was in 2012. In the middle of the eighth inning, the game was tied. The spotlight shone on the last row of Section 219, the regular seat of Journey's lead singer, San Francisco native Steve Perry. As the piano intro started, he stood. The crowd cheered and rose, and Perry led the stadium in a sing-along. That year we did not stop believin' and the Giants won the World Series.

The memory brought on that familiar sensation of tightness in my throat and the back of my eyes, my nerves reacting to grief. It's curious how the body synchronizes perfectly with the mind, just like the crowd did with Steve Perry.

I put my sneakers on the dashboard, something Alan hates. He let it slide because I was staring out the car window, not bothering to wipe the tears. COVID-19 had changed everything and it wasn't finished.

On the other side of Potrero Hill, the food bank volunteers motioned us to a large plastic crate filled with bags of food. We checked in, then loaded fifteen heavy bags into the car.

"Thank you," said one of the volunteers.

"Thank *you*," we replied. We were only delivering food for a couple of hours. Many of them were working seven days a week to make sure nobody went hungry.

Our deliveries began in the Excelsior, one of the many San Francisco neighborhoods we'd heard of but never visited. "Fun fact," I said to Alan, "the streets here were named after the capitals of countries by a man called Emanuel Lewis, who was instrumental in the Excelsior's development after the 1906 earthquake."

"Don't distract me, I'm trying to navigate here," Alan said affectionately.

He is used to my jabbering while he drives. But we were in unfamiliar territory, the route full of turns and the roads hilly. I stopped talking and started scanning the street for our destination on the right.

A bright blue house with a sunny yellow door was our first stop. I pressed the doorbell twice, placed the bag of food on the stoop, and stepped back. Social distancing prevented us from helping the seniors carry the food into their homes even if they were too frail to carry a fifteen-pound bag.

A minute later, the door slowly opened. A small elderly Asian woman looked warily through the screen.

"I'm from the food bank." I held up the badge hanging around my neck and pointed at the food.

She broke into a smile. "Thank you thank you," she said. I went back to the car with a lighter step.

Following this was a woman who clasped her hands and said, "Oh, this is for me."

Halfway through our deliveries, we met a Latina *abuela* in a purple bathrobe and matching fluffy slippers. She blew thank-you kisses to Alan, waiting in the car, and this man known for his British stoicism rolled down the window and enthusiastically waved back.

There's a difference between hearing, "They were so happy to get the food," and experiencing it for yourself.

Our last stop was a house with worn wooden steps lined with plants. There I met an older gentleman dressed for the day in gray pressed slacks, a white collared shirt, and pale blue cardigan even though he couldn't leave his house. At the sight of the food, his glittering eyes disappeared into a joyful grin. He reminded me of my favorite uncle who died a couple of years ago.

We drove home with the car windows down. The sun was out. My feet were on the floorboards. My arms were in the air. "Don't Stop Believin'" blasted through the car. We sang at the top of our lungs.

Now we spend every Saturday delivering food, exchanging more than a greeting with people we'll never meet again. We experience a momentary touchpoint, where we get a glimpse into each other's lives. I take away a longing for relatives who are gone but also a reminder that no matter how old you are, there is someone older, someone who carries a comforting strength and wisdom. Many of these seniors weigh less a hundred pounds and yet they lift heavy bags of food and offer simple gratitude that quells our fears.

The pandemic will end. We don't know what lies ahead, only

what we've left behind. But we will take into that unknown future the smiles, the air kisses, the thanks, and the gift of hope.

Shana Mahaffey is the author of *Sounds Like Crazy*. She lives in San Francisco with two cats and her husband and is a cofounder of the Castro Writers' Cooperative.

HOPE SINGS

By Ana Hebra Flaster

I call Papi every night so he can talk. My father's pretty deaf, so it's easier if I just listen to these forty-five-minute nightly monologues. Sometimes, I forget and try to ask a question. Usually, it's easy to lose myself in Papi's stories about our old lives in Cuba and his years of playing Triple-A baseball in the U.S. My goal is to distract him, keep his mind off COVID-19, the turmoil roiling in our country, the hate—the uncertainty of it all. This cocktail of woe reminds him of another time in his life when his world fell apart.

My parents fled Cuba—and the revolution they'd once supported—in 1967, when I was five years old. We arrived in the U.S. as political refugees and ended up in Nashua, New Hampshire. The state motto, "Live Free or Die," sounded like a hymn to my parents. It was also comforting that Canada was so close they could almost see the border. If communism spread to the U.S., they'd have a way out. Once you've lived through a revolution gone awry, you always have a Plan B.

Papi lives just a few towns north of Nashua now. He's eighty-seven years old, a grieving widower and former factory worker, living alone in a town with almost no Latinos and only a handful of people who understand his wacky English. Mami was nine years younger, but the universe didn't care. She died six years ago, another beautiful soul snatched by the cancer bitch. So Papi lives on his memories, Meals on Wheels, and visits from family and old friends.

As the oldest child, I've taken on the role of supreme fixer. I solve problems real and imagined, boss my brother and sister around, and try to guide Papi toward health and contentment. Even before the pandemic, this was like riding a sidewinder missile. He did what he wanted to do—ate too much too fast, dehydrated himself regularly, stopped taking medicine just because, climbed ladders, tinkered with every electrical gadget and motor not just in his house but in his neighbors'. Since the pandemic, I explain, I remind, I pester—to no avail. He forgets his gloves and mask. He visits people who also disrespect the new rules and let him right on in. I've almost stopped trying to keep him safe. Almost. I sneak reminders into our calls when I can, knowing it's nearly pointless.

Before I can pretend to have our nightly conversation tonight, I have to get him to turn down the TV, which he keeps at an earsplitting volume. I cup my hand over the speaker and yell: "¡*Baja el volumen!*"

He shouts back, "¿*Qué?* ¿*Qué?*" but eventually comes up with the same idea. "Wait a minute," he yells, "let me turn this thing down."

That's when I hear them, trilling, harmonizing with each other, their songs cascading through the air. Papi's forty-something canaries are belting out their evening song for the world to hear. The house sounds like a rain forest—chirps, peeps, flapping wings, whistles—a nightly chorus that's keeping Papi alive during this season of pain.

———

Just before my mother died, she approved my suggestion that she let Papi breed canaries again. He'd done it as a side hustle to bring in extra money in the '70s, but Mami started to complain when the number of birds approached one hundred. He loved them too much to sell them, it turned out. Mami kept after him to reduce the size of the flock, and he sold them all. After she died, we encouraged him to start breeding them again, but Papi couldn't bring himself to think about canaries. They reminded him of happier days.

My brother snuck a canary into the house, pretending it was a gift for his daughter who was away at school. Could Papi take care of it until she returned from college? Papi didn't stand a chance. He bought a few more the following week. The breeding began, and in no time, he had a small flock of healthy yellow, white, and red fluff balls in a floor-to-ceiling aviary in his basement. He kept detailed charts, noting who sang to whom, which females carried straw in their beaks—a sign that they wanted to nest—which males fed their girlfriends broccoli treats, which fathers and mothers were attentive to their chicks. He walked up and down the basement stairs all day long and got in shape again. He had beautiful, innocent beings to protect and nurture. And they sang to him every night.

The canaries lifted him through, if not out of, his grief, and we started to see a glimmer of the old Papi. But after the virus hit, and then the racial unrest, something in Papi started to wither. He talked more about the darkest days after the revolution, when everything turned upside down and the impossible notion of leaving family and home behind forever hardened into something real. Then he announced he was going to sell the birds. All of them. I couldn't let that happen. How would he fill his days? How would he keep grief and fear at a safe distance?

———

Papi is on the phone, winding into a new story now, something about a game he pitched in Gainesville in 1955, when he played on the Washington Senators farm team. I sneak in a question, asking if he's complying with the COVID protection rules.

"*Sí, sí, sí,*" he says. "You must drive your husband crazy. Hey, did I tell you I sold ten canaries to the Portuguese guy down the street?"

"What? When?"

"Today. He and his good-for-nothing son-in-law came over. I don't like that guy. Anyway, I got thirty dollars apiece for the birds. I gave them some star singers…"

I don't ask if anyone wore a mask because I know the answer, and he knows I'm mad about it. I take a deep breath.

Papi sighs. "Oh, come on. They weren't here long. We just had a little Cuban coffee in the kitchen—they loved it. Looked at the birds. I gave them some seed just to get them started."

I try, but it's no use. I can't keep it in. I yell into the phone, "You don't sell canaries in the middle of a pandemic!"

"Why not?" he shouts. "I can't live the way you want. I have to do something! You have to leave me alone!"

So it goes for a while, and then we stop as a single canary lets loose a bright pink explosion of song that fills Papi's house and soars through the ether into my ears. Neither one of us talk. We barely breathe, mesmerized by the beauty of the music and the spirit of the creature that is singing.

Finally, the canary's song dies down, and I dare to ask my question. "Papi, are you going to sell them all?"

"Who said I was selling the birds? You kids are always dramatizing everything."

I don't want to remind him that he was the one who brought it up, adamantly. That had been a particularly bad news night, with a new surge of virus cases in the South, more looting, another black man dead after a confrontation with Atlanta police. We wondered out loud to each other, trying to make sense of this new world. After a long pause, he said, "I'm selling my birds. Every single one… What's the point?"

I should have remembered that life pulls us along, sometimes kicking and dragging, to the next day. We'd crawled out of the darkness after Mami died, thinking we'd never make it. Yet here we are. Facing new pains, uncertainties, and fears. Papi had only threatened to sell his canaries in that bleak moment as we watched the news. Hope had gone someplace else. Now it was back. And the canary in the basement knew it before we did.

ANA HEBRA FLASTER is a Cuban American whose work has appeared in the *New York Times*, *The Boston Globe*, and *The Boston Globe Magazine*, among other publications. Her essays have been featured on NPR's *All Things Considered* and the Suitcase Stories/PBS series *Stories From The Stage*.

TELL ME A STORY

By Michelle Wildgen

My daughter keeps asking me for stories. Every time we take a walk to a park near our home, which we do a few times a day to break up the quarantine monotony, Holly requests a story. But where I once had a ready supply, now I have a fallow field.

"I don't have any good ideas right now," I admit to her, and she sighs.

It's surprising how rarely I have used my storytelling skills in nine years of parenting. Once, when she was two and a half, I found myself panicked and unmoored because I had Holly on my lap on a night-time flight with no lighting and no access to electronic devices. How the hell was I supposed to occupy this wide-awake child as we sat in the dark? Maybe it did not take quite as long as it feels in my memory before some voice inside my head murmured, "You're a professional storyteller, you idiot," but it felt like a long time.

Even then, I just whispered fairy tales to her, never feeling as confident a parent as I do a professional. But maybe that moment opened a door.

Slowly, as Holly grew older, other stories emerged. There was an ongoing series about Chester the Whipped-Cream Bandit, a small, balding mustachioed man who travels from town to town convincing gullible municipalities to throw enormous whipped cream-based events, so he can make off with their whipped cream supply and eat it. Then we moved on to McGillicuddy, a ten-year-old who is forever embarking upon massive projects that always get out of hand. He has reinvented holiday meals, co-chaired neighborhood snow-building competitions, fashion shows, and Easter egg hunts. He's pure id, with endless energy, no social boundaries, and I think of him as part trickster god, part Amelia Bedelia, and part David Bowie. The costuming is the most important part of a McGillicuddy story, but food also plays a major role. Holly can tell when I'm hungry and uninspired because the story devolves into a series of elaborate descriptions of things she knows I'd like to eat.

The McGillicuddy stories used to be a way to pass the time on our walks to and from school. Then, when she was in the hospital with shigella, we asked a little more of him. It was McGillicuddy who got us through a few IV insertions and other distresses by taking over the zoo for a week, where he did things like give neck rubs to the giraffes and offer whiteboards and markers to the chimpanzees, who used them to plot out intra-primate warfare. (We were having a hard week. Things went dark.)

It's shockingly simple, this ancient process that requires nothing except me talking with my daughter, telling her stuff I literally pull out of thin air. I never babysat, never quite knew what to do with a baby or a toddler, and embarked on the work of raising a child counting on my husband to have a clue where I didn't, yet amid all that other uncertainty, I can do this for her.

It occurs to me that although I have spent almost my entire life devoted to stories, a part of me cannot believe this actually works.

But as I said, I've had a hard time lately knowing what stories to tell her. I'm fried by all the same things everyone is, and sections of my brain may have shut down over these past weeks and months. But part of the problem is just despair. I often think that if I were making the choice about whether to have kids now, instead of back in 2010, I wouldn't do it. Not because I have any regret about having my daughter here, but because I have lost a lot of my optimism about our ability to face challenges, to choose productive leaders, to hear each other, and to act in others' interest or even our own.

But she is here now. She has big brown eyes, a gift for climbing trees, porch railings, and rock walls, and an insanely vexing habit of mixing up potions and leaving them all around the house to become murky jars of pond water and expensive, wasted spices. Her pixie cut has grown out in quarantine into a sort of surfer-boy cut. I once asked her to invent the worst name in the world and her answer, almost immediately, was "Pubert Squelch." She is here, and she is in my face twenty-three hours a day, but hers is so beautiful that I'm going to let that slide.

We go for the one thousandth walk of the spring, stopping at a brace of trees that she has climbed roughly three thousand times. She is getting a little bored with them, but gamely she persists.

Then we keep walking and she asks me for a McGillicuddy story. I love it that this ridiculous creation matters to her. I fear that if I try to write it all down, it'll dampen his anarchic silliness. And after each workday of living inside other people's stories, that particular part of my brain—which starts off full of electricity and juice—can wind up dead as sand.

But then I wonder if perhaps these stories don't use the same geography after all. It seems possible that a totally different part of my brain is responsible for conjuring up McGillicuddy lounging under the Christmas tree, drinking milk from a wine goblet. I haven't actually researched this, but it would make sense if, from that other, more hopeful little cluster of synapses, there springs some kind of vision for what could be, some belief that we can still achieve it.

"I'm not sure if I have any new ideas for a McGillicuddy story," I tell her.

"I'll give you ideas," she says. Then she does, and they are exactly what I need.

MICHELLE WILDGEN'S novels include *You're Not You* and *Bread and Butter*. Her work has appeared in the *New York Times*; *O, the Oprah Magazine*; *Best Food Writing*; and various anthologies and literary journals. She is currently at work on her fourth novel.

GLITTER ROAD

By January Gill O'Neil

I'll take my miracles however they appear
these days—a salamander poking its head

above the bricks; the shocking blue overcoat
of the season's first bluebird; a spider web

unbroken. At the corner of Molly Barr
and McElroy I saw a thick trail of glitter

in the curve of the right turn lane. Fuchsia.
Heavy shimmer refracting the noonday sun

as if laying flat a rainbow's extracted hue.
Not paint, or blood, or a parade shedding

its cheer. It's the faded streak of eye shadow
as it trails into flecks, then disappears.

I think of cars passing through this moment—
their undercarriages aglow with possibility.

Hard not to feel good riding a glistening wave,
my tires now bespeckled with a purple sheen

that's tough to rid or wash away, the road ahead
made beautiful by this temporary shine.

JANUARY GILL O'NEIL is an associate professor at Salem State University, and the author of *Rewilding* (2018), *Misery Islands* (2014), and *Underlife* (2009), all published by CavanKerry Press. From 2019-2020, she served as the John and Renée Grisham Writer-in-Residence at the University of Mississippi, Oxford.

NEEDLECAST

By Robin Black

i.

Five spruce, none more than four feet tall. Six years ago we planted them on the lawn that rolls down from our house. A miniature grove of bluish trees, pudgy, squat, all nestled close, a genial coven. You could imagine fairy tales unfolding there among those wee beings. You could imagine them joining hands—joining branches—and circling in a jolly dance.

The first to die went quickly. One day last summer, we both saw it, suddenly, as though it had only just appeared like that: browned and denuded, unmistakably too far gone. It was a skeleton before we noticed that it had sickened. This can't have happened overnight, though it seemed that way. Maybe neither of us could see the damage until it was that extreme because when we looked at the grove, we were blinded by what it meant to us, by our story of it. Our happy, magical trees! (There are times for us all when we see our own hearts, no matter what we view.) But now, undeniably, this was a dying tree. It was a dead tree.

And then last fall, another. And then a third. With these last ones, though, we saw the unmistakable early burnishing of rust toward the trunk, a shadowy death-sentence hue.

One, two, three. Gone.

ii.

Gone.

This morning, as I write, the official number of American dead has passed ninety thousand. *Ninety thousand dead. Ninety thousand dead. Ninety thousand dead. Ninety thousand dead.* Like a word repeated so many times it ceases to convey its meaning, these numbers numb us, have numbed me. *Ninety thousand dead.* One lost life can be unbearable—even when the person is a stranger. But how do you grieve ninety thousand deaths? How do you open your heart to that pain, hold onto the humanity lost?

iii.

It wasn't only the spruce trees.

Also last summer, the lavender failed us *en masse* after thriving for years. Turkey vultures began congregating on our fence each morning, in seemingly ominous conversations. The snakes revealed themselves to us, in the grass, on our paths, atop the dead gray lavender, in numbers we had never seen before.

Something is wrong, I thought then.

Now I know I was right.

Our house is a lovely place in which to pass a pandemic. We are surrounded by farmers, which means we are surrounded by normalcy still. Cows grazing. Machines whirring. Roosters crowing. Crops growing.

Maybe if I didn't live in a place so outwardly unaffected by this, I wouldn't see magical portents and signs everywhere.

Fairy-tale logic.

Even the bird mistaking his reflection for a rival, tapping incessantly at our windowed door, seems at times more magic than flesh, a malevolent spirit sent to break the seal on our isolation.

iv.

But there are ways in which I want that seal broken.

Ninety thousand Americans dead. One hundred thousand dead.

Numbers we have never seen before.

It is important, I believe, to feel the pain of these deaths—especially for those of us who are unscathed. I have lost no one. (Not yet.) I could pass my days in a kind of uninformed, privileged fog. But soon it will be one hundred thousand dead. (The more I say it, the less real it feels, like an incantation that weakens with every use.) *One hundred thousand dead.* It is possible, I know, to be seduced by the incomprehensibility of that figure, of the even higher figures to come. And I do not want that. I believe it is immoral, yes, but also unhealthy—emotionally, spiritually—to bear witness to this tragedy and not feel its ache.

We are cut off here, in our country home, but I want to be connected to the truth of this time, not escape into this escape of ours, among the trees.

v.

I learn the word for what killed our spruce: *Needlecast.* A fairy-tale word for my fairy-tale trees. A spell was cast: *Needlecast.*

"Why did two of them survive?"

My expert shrugs. "There's a lot we don't know," he says.

The remaining trees are a strange study in contrasts. One is classic, a perfectly symmetrical Christmas tree. The picture of health. The other is gnarled, twisted, an against-all-odds survivor, by all appearances the one of the original five that should have died first.

There is indeed a lot we don't know.

"Needlecast." I say it out loud.

vi.

Fairy-tale logic, it turns out, is not wrong logic—it is the logic of poetry; it is metaphor; it is the music of fiction. And sometimes it is what leads us to a greater understanding of others' pain.

One day, I look down the lawn toward those three skeletal remains and I see:

The elderly woman dying alone in her nursing home.

The doctor unable to save his third patient that day.

The child whose father has just been placed on a ventilator.

(There are times for us all when we see our own hearts, no matter what we view.)

vii.

Ninety thousand dead. One hundred thousand dead . . .

Once upon a time, a terrible spell was cast . . .

viii.

I tell my husband that I want to replant the grove around the two remaining trees. And I want variety, not so much for aesthetics, but for protection. (I don't tell him that I want the survivors to have company, that I don't want them left so alone, that I want to *cheer up our trees*.) We choose a Japanese maple, a lilac, a globe Scotch pine, a cryptomeria, a Vanderwolf pine, a dappled willow. . .

And I am something strangely like glad when I realize that the sight of this new grove, the memory of what it used to be, the sight of the survivors, can still bring me to tears.

Once upon a time, a terrible spell was cast . . .

(Ninety thousand dead. A hundred thousand dead . . .)

Meanwhile we are doing what we need to do.

We are adapting.

We are pushing forward.

We are reconfiguring.

We are working on comprehending.

We are distancing.

We are reaching out.

We are grieving.

And we are planting trees. In numbers we have never seen before.

R OBIN B LACK is the author most recently of the novel *Life Drawing* and the collection *Crash Course: Essays from Where Writing and Life Collide*. At work on her second novel, she teaches in the Rutgers-Camden MFA Program.

WE WEAR THE MASK

By W. Ralph Eubanks

let them only see us, while
We wear the mask.
    —Paul Laurence Dunbar, "We Wear the Mask"

It was on the once-peopled streets of Manhattan in early March of 2020 that I noticed something out of the ordinary. There they were on the edge of Bryant Park: three patches of a pale blue once associated with hospitals and operating rooms, partially covering the faces of three fashionably dressed women. This trio pierced my consciousness so completely that I surreptitiously snapped a photograph I posted the photo to my Instagram feed, dubbing it "Springtime in New York." "You're a regular Bill Cunningham," a friend commented. I smiled proudly at that, yet as the day went on, I became more mournful than pleased with the photo.

While I would never call myself a photographer, I have long been a student of the medium. In my course on the image of the American South, I constantly remind my students that what we see and how we see it is not a passive act. The reason I even thought to document that moment was because of my love of photography, which had also taken me to New York that March, to see a Dorothea Lange exhibition at the Museum of Modern Art.

In a 1966 interview, Lange recalled that in her work as a photographer for the Farm Security Administration during the Great Depression, she was given no specific instruction on what to photograph, other than to "see what is really there." What she saw were faces. "The human face is the universal language," Lange proclaimed. "The same expressions are understandable and readable all across the world." Lange's photographs weren't just about the human face but the human condition. She photographed the wounded, the defeated, the alienated, all tightly captured and perfectly composed. "It's not pictorial illustration, it's evidence," Lange once said of her work. "It's a record of human experience. It's linked with history."

When I left the museum and returned to the streets of New York, I began to notice more people in masks. As the day wore on, I realized they were all Asian. That was when an unsettled feeling flowed over me. I remembered that just a month before, an Asian woman was attacked in the New York City subway for wearing a mask. Asians were also being attacked when not wearing masks, having been labeled as the carriers and cause of the pandemic. On the train ride back to Washington, when I once again witnessed only Asians wearing masks, I began to realize this was not mere happenstance.

Now, we all wear the mask. The visage of almost everyone in my neighborhood in Washington, DC, is shielded by a piece of paper or cloth of varying designs and colors. As Dorothea Lange reminded me that day in New York, the human face is the universal language. But now that visual language is partially hidden. Smiles, excitement, or despair are all shielded by a piece of cloth. In a short time, a mask moved from a rarity on the street, something worn by one segment of our population to shield them from xenophobia, to being another part of the landscape. Its sordid history is still known, but now is largely forgotten.

With everyone masked, I have begun to wonder if we can still see what is really there. Or even remember what was once there.

———

Like every Black person in America, before I ever had to wear a physical mask, I sometimes donned a figurative one. My mask didn't grin and lie, as the poet Paul Laurence Dunbar described. But it did shield the truth. I used my mask to carefully shroud my dread and anger about the racism I encountered every day.

The first time I heard Dunbar's poem "We Wear the Mask" was at a school assembly at my then-segregated school during what was then known as Negro History Week. I was only twelve and not exactly sure what the poem meant. What is human guile? I wondered. And what is the writer hiding from? Two years later, in my early days of inhabiting the burning house known as school integration in Mississippi, I learned what it meant to wear the mask, albeit one of my own design. Rather than showing the pain I felt at the unequal treatment and sometimes benign neglect by some of my teachers, I soldiered on. I conditioned myself to keep inside whatever I truly felt. My face was shielded by the books I read constantly, which helped me develop an interior life that shielded me from the indignities of the racism I faced at school. I wore the mask.

Years later, when I was asked to give a speech at my high school, I began by reading Dunbar's poem. That day I confessed what it felt like to keep my emotions bottled up during my high school years. "No one here should ever feel they need to wear the mask," I reminded them. Given the somewhat tepid response to the poem, I was not sure whether my message got across. Then, as I looked out at the crowd, I observed that the demographics of the school had changed. The school was now largely Black, with a mere smattering of whites, mostly those who were too poor to attend the nearby, largely white private academy. Next I learned that more than three quarters of the students were on free or reduced lunch. Re-segregation comes with its own set of issues surrounding equality and fairness. The mask I spoke of might not have mirrored their experiences.

That speech was more than a decade ago and those young people in the audience are all adults. Many of them still live in my little town, navigating the COVID-19 pandemic in a state showing no mercy to the poor and vulnerable. The inequities I saw that day are most certainly magnified by this crisis. Mississippi public policy seems to have morphed into a modern-day version of eugenics blended with social Darwinism. It feels like an attempt to eradicate people living in poverty by neglect. Welfare funds totaling $94 million were embezzled in a complex scheme that robbed the poor to enhance the lives of the powerful. Those who have power are able to protect themselves with masks and protective gear, while those at risk—who are largely Black and poor, uninsured, and with insecure access to food and healthcare—are simply left to languish and die.

Today we may all be required to wear the mask. But our masks are unequal.

———

Seeing is a way of knowing, how we gather evidence and make sense of our lives. My past life in Mississippi and the divided life I now live between my home state and my adopted hometown of Washington, DC, affects everything I see. While on the surface it seems as if these two places have little in common, both locales have stark inequities within their borders. You can live in Washington and never go to poor neighborhoods like Anacostia, just like Mississippians can avoid the Delta and its visibly impoverished people and landscape. Both places sequester the least powerful in a separate realm.

When I walk through my rapidly gentrifying neighborhood in Washington, I see people with masks and without masks. It's something I watch for on the long meditative walks that have become necessary for me to maintain some illusion of sanity. But whether or not the person is wearing a mask, rules of social distancing are always observed, so I believe my unmasked neighbors know the threat of the virus is real. But for some unknown reason, they seem unable to shift their lives in a way that acknowledges that things have changed.

It makes me wonder what life will be like once we no longer need to wear the mask. During these times when I must hide my face, I have become keenly aware of the inequalities this crisis has revealed. I try even harder to see not what I want to see, but what is really there. Yet when I think of those who act as if nothing has changed, I wonder if they see what I see. Is the mask covering their eyes? And as much as I worry about encountering this seemingly invisible virus, I worry about what else we Americans are not seeing.

W. RALPH EUBANKS is the author of *Ever Is a Long Time: A Journey into Mississippi's Dark Past*, *The House at the End of the Road*, and *A Place Like Mississippi* (forthcoming). He is a visiting professor of English and Southern Studies at the University of Mississippi.

ELEUTHERIA

By Major Jackson

There was so little to say of the iridescent grackles
above the court house or the architecture
of secrets below like a fragile vocabulary,
or the inundation of idols when winter thawed,
whatever was hidden out of loneliness.
But, what if we were changed at least once by nights of rain,
by drunken bees in a glade of tufted vetch,
by the fly-tormented psalms of Blake
edging further into the breath of our knowing?
This is a country with a single dream—
all the counties and all the town meetings and all
the demonstrations amount to a sole creation.
Last night I pictured our shadows liberated from human forms.
How do we know the color of freedom?
I've a face the shade of maple pressed like an encyclic leaf
in a book from another century no one reads.
I am imagining your fingernails, the great potential
of your profile, how you may never hear the gentlest
parts of my tumbling out of clouds:
sometimes we call it beauty, we, the martyrs.

MAJOR JACKSON is the award-winning author of five books of poetry, most recently *The Absurd Man* (2020), and serves as the poetry editor of the *Harvard Review*. He lives in South Burlington, Vermont, where he is the Richard A. Dennis Professor of English and University Distinguished Professor at the University of Vermont.

ACKNOWLEDGMENTS

It has truly taken a village to create this book. At the top of my gratitude list is Michelle Halket at Central Avenue Publishing. Not only is she a savvy and creative publisher, she is a transparent and trustworthy partner who puts one hundred percent of her energy into bringing books she believes in to market. I learned this two years ago, when CAP published my debut novel, *In the Shadow of 10,000 Hills*. I had no hesitation calling to ask if she would be interested in publishing an anthology to raise money for booksellers hit hard by the COVID economy. What I didn't anticipate was that Michelle would not only donate her time and services, but also reach out to IPG Distribution and other business partners to do the same.

I want to thank all of the ninety (as of this morning!) contributing authors for telling their stories with tenderness, honesty, and grace. Everyone was a pleasure to work with—not easy to say about ninety authors! And then there were those who went above and beyond: Michelle Wildgen was my partner in shaping these stories and the book. Laura Stanfill, publisher extraordinaire at Forest Avenue Press, offered guidance as well as reading the first set of pieces. Faith Adiele, Andrea King Collier, Sonora Jha, and Devi S. Laskar connected me with other authors in their communities to help ensure diverse representation. Jennie Shortridge and Garth Stein, both exemplary literary citizens in my Seattle community and just plain nice humans, lent their talent and support early on and throughout this project in numerous ways. Other early supporters were Jenna Blum, Gina Frangello, Lise Haines, Caroline Leavitt, Anna Quinn, Dawn Raffel, Sandra Sarr, Dani Shapiro, Steve Yarbrough, Lidia Yuknavitch, and Luis Alberto Urrea (the godfather of this Lovely Monster).

Special thanks to Susan Henderson, who reviewed the final manuscript and wrote her essay while fighting off the virus and grieving the death of her father. She has been one of my literary angels since I met her at the Community of Writers Summer Writing Workshop fifteen years ago, and is one of the most gifted and generous humans I know.

Finally, my endless gratitude goes to independent booksellers across the country. Some of my most joyous moments as a reader and author have been in the audience and on the stage in your stores, drinking coffee with friends in your cafes. I look forward to discovering new voices on your shelves again.

And I thank you, dear readers, for opening your hearts and minds to all of our stories. As Kwame Alexander so eloquently said, we need to keep sharing our experiences and listening. As David Sheff said, grief is fuel for taking compassionate action. Please, don't stop.

Jennifer Haupt, Editor

Please visit alonetogetherthebook.com for more information about the contributors to this collection, and our business partners who have provided services at a deep discount or free of charge. (Website designed by Abigail Carter Designs.)

NOTES

"Beyond All That" was originally published in the *Tupelo Quarterly*.

"Dayenu: Dispatches from the COVID-19 Sick Ward" was originally published in *Lilith Blog*.

"Today When I Could Do Nothing" was originally published in the *San Francisco Chronicle*.

"Sibling Estrangement and Social Distancing" was originally published on the *Psychology Today* blog, One True Thing.

"The Flow Room" was originally published in WBUR's *Cognoscenti*.

A version of "Searching for Grace During Lockdown" was originally published on the *Psychology Today* blog, One True Thing.

"The Inescapable Joy of Motherhood" was originally published on the *Psychology Today* blog, One True Thing.

"Pandemic Date Night" originally appeared, under a different title, in *The Nervous Breakdown*.

"America the Beautiful Again" was reprinted with kind permission from Beacon Press, from the book *How to Love a Country*.

"what to bring to a die-in" was originally published in *Winter Tangerine*.

"Billow of Thistles" was originally published in *Mumble Magazine*.

A version of "Celebrating in the Present Tense" was originally published in *USA Today*.

"Song at the End of the Mind" was previously published in *Pangyrus*.

"Disaster Unpreparedness" was originally published in *McSweeney's* as "The Disaster I Had Been Trained to Expect Happened to My Daughter."

"Shedding" was originally published in the *Rx Poetry Series* at Headline Poetry & Press.

"The House With The Mossy Roof" was previously published in *Stories from Seattle, Seattle Magazine.*

"Dear O" was previously published in *The Rumpus.*

ABOUT

Editor Jennifer Haupt's essays and articles have been published in *O, The Oprah Magazine; Parenting; The Rumpus; Spirituality & Health; The Sun* and many other publications. She also curates and edits the popular *Psychology Today* blog, "One True Thing," a collection of essays and interviews for authors and readers. Her debut novel, *In the Shadow of 10,000 Hills,* was awarded the Foreword Reviews Bronze Indie Award for Historical Fiction.

Content Editor/Copy Editor Michelle Wildgen, a longtime executive editor with the award-winning literary journal *Tin House*, is now a freelance editor and creative writing teacher in Madison, Wisconsin. Her novels include *You're Not You* and *Bread and Butter*. Her work has appeared in the *New York Times*; *O, the Oprah Magazine*; *Best Food Writing*; and various anthologies and literary journals. She is currently at work on her fourth novel.

Proofreader Molly Ringle studied language as a graduate student in linguistics, and has edited scientific papers, personal essays, and novels. She has published ten novels and novellas. Her next novel, *Lava Red Feather Blue,* comes out January 2021.

Ailsa Weisnewski has had a lifelong love and talent for art and illustration. She works professionally illustrating cards and books, and creating custom work for individuals and businesses. She lives in Seattle, Washington, and can be reached at ohhellohandmade.com.

Thank you for reading.

Books are a nation's treasure and those who curate
and collect them are invaluable parts of our society.

The net proceeds of this book are being donated to
the Book Industry Charitable Foundation which
provides assistance to bookstores in need.

Find out more about their amazing work at
bincfoundation.org

The audio and ebook editions contain bonus essays and poetry. Contributors include:

Alistair Bane

Misha Berson

Logan Blanton

Ewa Chrusciel

Greg Colucci

Elizabeth Dimarco

Sarah Domet

Deborah Green

Patricia Henley

Margot Kahn

Kathleen Kenneth

Eson Kim

Rebecca Mabanglo-Mayor

Catherine Matthews

McKenna Princing

Molly Ringle

Elizabeth Rosner

Michael Shou-Yung Shum

Donna Baier Stein

Jaclyn Watterson

Audiobook published by Podium Audio.

Faith Adiele, Kelli Russell Agodon, Kwame Alexander, Alistair Ba
Misha Berson, Robin Black, Richard Blanco, Logan Blanton, Jen
Blum, Gayle Brandeis, Sommer Browning, Abigail Carter, Clau
Castro Luna, Ewa Chrusciel, Meg Waite Clayton, Ching-In Ch
Serena Chopra, Andrea Collier, Greg Colucci, Elizabeth Dimar
Sarah Domet, Andre Dubus III, Teri Elam, W. Ralph Eubanks, Am
Flame, Ana Hebra Flaster, Jamie Ford, Gina Frangello, Julie Gardn
Nikki Giovanni, Michelle Goodman, Deborah Green, Lise Haines, Sa
Hassan, Jennifer Haupt, Christine Hemp, Susan Henderson, Patri
Henley, Jane Hirshfield, Pam Houston, Major Jackson, Scott Jam
Sonora Jha, Margot Kahn, Jessica Keener, Kathleen Kenneth, Le
Khalaf Tuffaha, Stephen P. Kiernan, Eson Kim, Sally Koslow, Je
Kwok, Devi S. Laskar, Ada Limón, Caroline Leavitt, Roberto Lova
Rebecca Mabanglo-Mayor, Shana Mahaffey, Catherine Matthe
Donna Miscolta, Dinty W. Moore, January Gill O'Neil, Paule
Perhach, McKenna Princing, Ruben Quesada, Anna Quinn, Peter
Quinn, Dawn Raffel, Susan Rich, Molly Ringle, Elizabeth Rosn
Jennifer Rosner, Kevin Sampsell, Sandra Sarr, Dani Shapiro, Da
Sheff, David Shields, N. L. Shompole, Michael Shou-Yung Shum, Jen
Shortridge, Laura Stanfill, Donna Baier Stein, Garth Stein, Meli
Studdard, Grace Talusan, Martha Anne Toll, Luis Alberto Urr
Jaclyn Watterson, Michelle Wildgen, Steve Yarbrough, Krist
Millares Young, Lidia Yuknavitch, Faith Adiele, Kelli Russ
Agodon, Kwame Alexander, Alistair Bane, Misha Berson, Robin Bla
Richard Blanco, Logan Blanton, Jenna Blum, Gayle Brandeis, Somm
Browning, Abigail Carter, Claudia Castro Luna, Ewa Chrusci
Meg Waite Clayton, Ching-In Chen, Serena Chopra, Andrea Coll
Greg Colucci, Elizabeth Dimarco, Sarah Domet, Andre Dubus
Teri Elam, W. Ralph Eubanks, Amber Flame, Ana Hebra Flast
Jamie Ford, Gina Frangello, Julie Gardner, Nikki Giovanni, Miche
Goodman, Deborah Green, Lise Haines, Sadia Hassan, Jennifer Hau
Christine Hemp, Susan Henderson, Patricia Henley, Jane Hirshfie
Pam Houston, Major Jackson, Scott James, Sonora Jha, Margot Ka
Jessica Keener, Kathleen Kenneth, Lena Khalaf Tuffaha, Steph
P. Kiernan, Eson Kim, Sally Koslow, Jean Kwok, Devi S. Laskar, A
Limón, Caroline Leavitt, Roberto Lovato, Rebecca Mabanglo-May
Shana Mahaffey, Catherine Matthews, Donna Miscolta, Dinty
Moore, January Gill O'Neil, Paulette Perhach, McKenna Princi
Ruben Quesada, Anna Quinn, Peter G. Quinn, Dawn Raffel, Susan Ri
Molly Ringle, Elizabeth Rosner, Jennifer Rosner, Kevin Sampse
Sandra Sarr, Dani Shapiro, David Sheff, David Shields, N. L. Shompo
Michael Shou-Yung Shum, Jennie Shortridge, Laura Stanf
Donna Baier Stein, Garth Stein, Melissa Studdard, Grace Talus
Martha Anne Toll, Luis Alberto Urrea, Jaclyn Watterson, Miche
Wildgen, Steve Yarbrough, Kristen Millares Young, Lidia Yuknavi